BREEDING AND RAISING HORSES

By

M. E. Ensminger, *collaborator,*

Animal Science Research Division,

Agricultural Research Service

UNITED STATES DEPARTMENT OF AGRICULTURE

Fredonia Books
Amsterdam, The Netherlands

Breeding and Raising Horses

by M. E. Ensminger

for U.S. Department of Agriculture

ISBN: 1-4101-0869-4

Copyright © 2005 by Fredonia Books

Reprinted from the 1972 edition

Fredonia Books
Amsterdam, The Netherlands
http://www.fredoniabooks.com

The breed pictures in this handbook were supplied by the following persons and organizations, listed in order of discussion of the several breeds

American Albino Association, Inc.
American Buckskin Registry Association
Krona Horse Farms
American Paint Horse Association
American Saddle Horse Breeders Association
Appaloosa Horse Club, Inc.
International Arabian Horse Association
Mr. A. Mackay-Smith
Mavis Connemara Farm
Galiceno Horse Breeders Association, Inc.
American Hackney Horse Society and Kennedy Pony Farm
Mrs. Margit Sigray Bessenyey
Missouri Fox Trotting Horse Breed Association, Inc.
American Morgan Horse Association, Inc.
Mr. Sam Roberts
Mr. George LaHood, Jr.
American Association of Owners and Breeders of Peruvian Paso Horses
Pinto Horse Association of America, Inc.
Pony of the Americas Club, Inc.
Mr. Lewis J. Moorman, Jr.
American Shetland Pony Club
Mr. Robert E. Brislawn
United States Trotting Association
Voice Publishing Co. (*Voice of the Tennessee Walking Horse*)
The Jockey Club
Welsh Pony Society of America, Inc.

CONTENTS

BREEDING AND RAISING HORSES

By M. E. ENSMINGER, collaborator, *Animal Science Research Division, Agricultural Research Service*

INTRODUCTION

Light horses and ponies have continued to increase in numbers and importance. Saddle clubs are growing in membership. Horse shows are increasing in size and number. More people are riding horses for pleasure than ever before. Projects in 4–H Horse Clubs outnumber projects in 4–H Beef Clubs.

On the western ranges, cow ponies are still used in the traditional manner; mechanical replacement has not yet been devised. Horseracing has become one of America's leading spectator sports.

Horses may be classified as light horses, ponies, or draft horses, according to size, build, and use.

Light horses stand 14–2 to 17 hands high (a hand is 4 inches). They weigh 900 to 1,400 pounds, and are used primarily for riding, driving, or racing, or for utility purposes on the farm. Light horses generally are more rangy and are capable of more action and greater speed than draft horses.

Ponies are under 14–2 hands high and weigh up to 900 pounds.

Draft horses stand 14–2 to 17–2 hands high. They weigh 1,400 pounds or more and are used primarily for drawing loads and for other heavy work.

Light horses and ponies are discussed in this handbook.

BREEDS AND THEIR CHARACTERISTICS

A breed of horses may be defined as a group of horses having a common origin and possessing certain well-defined, distinctive, uniformly transmitted characteristics that are not common to other horses.

The common breeds of light horses and ponies are discussed in the following list.[1]

---

[1] No person or department has authority to approve a breed. The only legal basis for recognizing a breed is contained in the Tariff Act of 1930, which provides for the duty-free admission of purebred breeding horses provided they are registered in the country of origin. But this applies to imported animals only. In this handbook, therefore, no official recognition of any breed is intended or implied. Rather, every effort has been made to present the factual story of the breeds. In particular, information about the new or less widely distributed breeds is needed and often difficult to obtain.

American Albino Horse

American Albino Horses, or American White Horses and Ponies, originated in the United States, in Naper, Nebr. They have snow-white hair, pink skin, and light blue, dark blue (near black), brown, or hazel eyes. The breed ranges from 8 to 17 hands high and includes both ponies and horses.

American Albinos are used as riding and utility horses. Their snow-white color makes them attractive as trained horses for exhibition purposes and as parade and flag bearer horses.

Animals are disqualified for registration if the color is pale cream or off white.

1

2

FIGURE 1.—American Albino stallion, "White Wings," first permanently registered stallion of the breed.

American Buckskin

American Buckskin horses originated in the United States. Coat colors are buckskin, red dun, or grulla (mouse-dun). They have a dorsal stripe, and usually a transverse stripe over the withers and shoulders and zebra-type stripes on the legs.

American Buckskins are used as stock horses, pleasure horses, and show horses.

Animals are disqualified for registration if they have white markings above the knees and hocks or white spots on the body.

FIGURE 2.—American Buckskin stallion, "Davis Poco Don," a champion in breeding and performance competition.

American Gotland Horse

American Gotland Horses originated on the Baltic island of Gotland, a part of Sweden. Coat colors are bay, brown, black, dun, chestnut, roan, or palomino, and some leopard and blanket markings. They average about 51 inches high, with a range of 11 to 14 hands.

American Gotland Horses are used for harness racing (trotting), as pleasure horses and jumpers, and as riding horses for children and medium sized adults.

Pintos and animals with large markings are disqualified for registration.

FIGURE 3.—American Gotland stallion, "Gulldson 40," sire of show, pleasure, jumping, and trot racing ponies.

American Paint Horse

American Paint Horses[2] originated in the United States. Coat colors are white plus any other color, but the coloring must be a recognizable paint. No discrimination is made against glass, blue, or light-colored eyes.

[2] Two different associations have evolved for the registration of these vari-colored horses. In the Pinto Horse Association of America, Inc., which is the older of the two registries, the breed is known as Pinto Horse, whereas in the American Paint Horse Association, the breed is known as the American Paint Horse. Both groups of horses are similar in color.

BN–32892

FIGURE 4.—American Paint Horse stallion, "Yellow Mount," first American Paint Horse Association champion and two-time National Champion Halter Stallion.

American Paint Horses are used as pleasure horses and for showing and racing.

Animals are disqualified for registration unless they have natural white markings above the knees or hocks, except on the face; if they have appaloosa coloring or breeding; if they are adult horses under 14 hands high; or if they are five-gaited horses.

American Saddle Horse

American Saddle Horses originated in the United States, in Fayette County, Ky. Coat colors are bay, brown, gray, chestnut, or black. Gaudy white markings are undesirable. Animals have a long, graceful neck and proud action. They furnish an easy ride with great style and animation.

American Saddle Horses are used as three- and five-gaited saddle horses, and as harness, pleasure, and stock horses.

Appaloosa

Appaloosa horses originated in the United States—in Oregon, Washington, and Idaho—from animals that first came from Fergana, Central Asia. They have variable coat coloring but usually there is white over the loin and hips, with round or egg-shaped dark spots on the white areas.

The eyes show more white than most breeds,

BN–32564

FIGURE 5.—American Saddle mare, "Plainview's Julia," twice winner of the five-gaited championship at the Kentucky State Fair.

the skin is mottled, and the hoofs are striped vertically black and white. Appaloosas are used as stock, parade, race, and pleasure horses.

Animals are disqualified for registration unless they have Appaloosa characteristics; if they have draft horse, pony, albino, or pinto breeding; if they are cryptorchids; or if they are under 14 hands high at maturity, which is 5 years old or more.

BN–32568

FIGURE 6.—Appaloosa stallion, "Little Navajo Joe," a champion stallion.

Arabian

Arabian horses originated on the Arabian Peninsula. Coat colors usually are bay, gray, or chestnut, and occasionally white or black. White marks on the head and legs are common. The skin is always dark.

These animals have a beautiful head, short coupling, docility, great endurance, and a gay way of going. They are used as saddle, stock, show, race, and pleasure horses.

BN-32557

FIGURE 7.—Arabian mare, "Dornaba," U.S. National Champion Mare and Canadian Champion Mare.

Cleveland Bay

Cleveland Bay horses originated in England, in the Cleveland district of Yorkshire. The coat color is always solid bay on the body and black on the legs. These horses are larger than most light horse breeds; they weigh from 1,150 to 1,400 pounds.

Cleveland Bays are used for riding, driving, and all kinds of farm work. They also are used in crossbreeding to produce heavyweight hunters.

Animals are disqualified for registration if they are any color but bay, although a few white hairs on the forehead are permissible.

Connemara Pony

Connemara Ponies originated on the west coast of Ireland. Coat colors usually are gray,

BN-32576

FIGURE 8.—Cleveland Bay stallion, "Cleveland Farnley."

black, bay, dun, brown, or cream, and occasionally roan or chestnut.

These ponies are heavy boned, hardy, and docile; the average height is 14 hands. They are used as jumpers, as show ponies under saddle

BN-32569

FIGURE 9.—Connemara Pony stallion, "Camus John's Gladiator."

or in harness, and as riding ponies for both adults and children.

Animals are disqualified for registration if they have piebald or skewbald coloring.

Galiceno

Galiceno horses originated in Galicia, a province in northwestern Spain. Horses of this lineage were first brought to America by the conquistadores, but these horses were not introduced to the United States as a breed until 1958. The most common coat colors are bay, black, chestnut (sorrel), dun (buckskin), gray, brown, or palomino.

At maturity, Galicenos are 12 to 13 hands high and weigh 625 to 700 pounds. They are used as riding horses.

Animals are disqualified for registration if they have albino, pinto, or paint coloring, or if they are cryptorchids or monorchids.

BN–32567

FIGURE 10.—Galiceno stallion, "Gray Badger," champion at the Southwestern Exposition and Fat Stock Show, Fort Worth, Tex.

Hackney

Hackney horses originated on the east coast of England, in Norfolk and adjoining counties. The most common colors are chestnut, bay, or brown, and occasionally roan or black. White marks are common and desirable.

In the show ring, custom decrees that Hackney horses and ponies be docked and have

BN–32825

FIGURE 11.—Hackney stallion, "May Day Creation," champion stallion and sire of champion ponies.

their manes pulled. They have a high natural action.

Hackneys are used as heavy harness or carriage horses and ponies, and for crossbreeding purposes to produce hunters and jumpers.

Hungarian Horse

Hungarian Horses are a very old breed that originated in Hungary. The coat may be any color, either broken or solid.

BN–32572

FIGURE 12.—Hungarian mare, "Hungarian Barna."

These horses have a unique combination of style and beauty with ruggedness. They are used as stock, cutting, and pleasure horses, as hunters and jumpers, and for trail riding.

Animals are disqualified for registration if they are cryptorchids or have glass eyes.

Missouri Fox Trotting Horse

Missouri Fox Trotting Horses originated in the United States, in the Ozark Hills of Missouri and Arkansas. They usually are sorrel but any color is accepted.

These horses are distinguished by the fox trot gait. They are used as pleasure and stock horses and for trail riding.

Animals are disqualified for registration if they cannot fox trot.

BN-32578

FIGURE 14.—Morgan stallion, "Rex's Major Monte."

BN-32579

FIGURE 13.—Missouri Fox Trotting Mare, "Bay Jeannie."

Morgan

Morgan horses originated in the United States, in New England. Coat colors are bay, brown, black, or chestnut; extensive white markings are uncommon.

Morgan horses are noted for their easy keeping qualities, endurance, and docility. They are used as saddle and stock horses.

Animals are disqualified for registration if they are wall eyed or have white markings above the knee or hock, except that white markings on the face are acceptable.

Palomino

Palomino horses originated in the United States from animals of Spanish extraction. These horses are golden colored. They have a light colored mane and tail of white, silver, or ivory; the mane and tail may not have more than 15 percent dark or chestnut hair. White markings on the face or below the knees are acceptable.

BN-32577

FIGURE 15.—Palomino stallion, "Mach I," a show champion and winning racehorse.

Palominos are used as stock, parade, pleasure, saddle, and harness horses.

Animals of draft horse or pony breeding and the offspring of piebald or albino breeding are not eligible for registration.

Paso Fino

Paso Fino horses[3] originated in the Caribbean area, where they have existed for over 400 years. They have been registered in stud books in Puerto Rico, Cuba, and Colombia.

The coat may be any color. Bay, chestnut, or black with white markings are most common. Occasionally, palominos and pintos appear. Paso Finos are used as pleasure, cutting, and

[3] In the United States, two different breed associations have evolved for the registration and promotion of horses of Paso Fino background. But each of the registries has slightly different standards. The American Paso Fino Pleasure Horse Association, Inc., calls its breed Paso Fino, whereas the American Association of Owners and Breeders of Peruvian Paso Horses calls its breed Peruvian Paso.

parade horses and for endurance riding and drill team work.

Paso fino is Spanish, meaning fine step. The paso fino gait may be described as a broken pace. The legs on the same side move together, but the hind foot strikes the ground a fraction of a second before the front foot, producing a four-beat gait.

Animals that do not possess the paso fino gait or do not trace directly to purebred Paso Fino ancestry are not eligible for registration.

Peruvian Paso

Peruvian Paso horses[4] originated in Peru. The coat may be any color, but solid colors are preferred.

These horses are naturally five gaited—walk, paso, trot, huachano (broken pace), and canter. They are used as pleasure, parade, and endurance horses.

Animals are disqualified for registration if they have light forequarters, coarseness, or extreme height.

BN-32566

FIGURE 16.—Paso Fino gelding, "Sortibras," champion on the Continent.

BN-32574

FIGURE 17.—Peruvian Paso stallion, "Broche del Oro."

Pinto Horse

Pinto Horses[5] originated in the United States from horses brought in by the conquistadores. The coat should be half color or colors and half white, with many spots well placed.

[4] See footnote 3.

[5] See footnote 2, p. 2.

The two distinct pattern markings are overo and tobiano. Overo is a colored horse with white areas extending upward from the belly and lower regions, and there may be other white markings; but in tobiano the white areas on the back extend downward, and there may be other white markings as well. Glass eyes are acceptable. The registry association has a separate registry for ponies and horses under 14 hands high.

Pintos are used for any light horse purpose, but especially as show, parade, pleasure, and stock horses.

FIGURE 18.—Pinto stallion, "Sabino Creek," a stock-horse type.

Pony of the Americas

Ponies of the Americas originated in the United States, in Mason City, Iowa. Their coloring is like the Appaloosa. They have white over the loin and hips and round or egg-shaped dark spots on the white areas.

These ponies have the characteristics of Arabian and Quarter Horses in miniature. They range in height from 46 to 54 inches and are used as western-type riding ponies for children.

Animals are disqualified for registration if they are not within the height range; do not have appaloosa coloring, including mottled skin and large whites of the eyes; if they have pinto markings; or if they are loud-colored roans.

BN–32894

FIGURE 19.—Pony of the Americas stallion, "Tomahawk's Big Creek," an international Grand Champion Stallion and a winning performance pony.

Quarter Horse

Quarter Horses originated in the United States. The most common colors are chestnut, sorrel, bay, or dun and sometimes black, palomino, roan, or brown.

These horses are well muscled and powerfully built; they have small, alert ears and sometimes heavily muscled cheeks and jaw. They are used as stock, race, and pleasure horses.

BN–32573

FIGURE 20.—Quarter Horse stallion, "Forecast," an American Quarter Horse Association champion and AAA racehorse.

Animals are disqualified for registration if they have pinto, appaloosa, or albino coloring or white markings on the underline.

Shetland Pony

Shetland Ponies originated in the Shetland Islands. The coat may be any color, either broken or solid.

These ponies are small. Two class sizes are recognized by the breed registry: (1) 43 inches and under and (2) 43 inches to 46 inches. They are used as mounts for children, harness and racing ponies, and roadsters.

Animals are disqualified for registration if they are over 46 inches high.

FIGURE 22.—Spanish Barb stallion, "Syndicate."

Standardbred

Standardbred horses originated in the United States. The most common colors are bay, brown, chestnut, or black and occasionally gray, roan, or dun.

Standardbreds are smaller, less leggy, and more rugged than Thoroughbreds. They are used for harness racing, either trotting or pacing, and as harness horses in horse shows.

FIGURE 21.—Shetland Pony stallion, "Curtiss Frisco Pete," winner of six consecutive grand championships at the National Shetland Congress.

Spanish Barb

Spanish Barbs originated in the United States, in Oshoto, Wyoming. The coat can be any color, solid or broken, except tobiano.

These horses have only five lumbar (loin region) vertebrae; most breeds have six. Also, they are characterized by short ears, a low-set tail, and round leg bones. They are used for trail riding and as cow ponies.

FIGURE 23.—Standardbred stallion, "Adios," leading sire of money winners of the breed.

10

Tennessee Walking Horse

Tennessee Walking Horses originated in the United States, in the Central Basin of Tennessee. Coat colors are sorrel, chestnut, black, roan, white, bay, brown, gray, or golden. White markings on the face and legs are common.

These horses are characterized by their running walk. They are used as plantation walking horses and as pleasure and show horses.

FIGURE 24.—Tennessee Walking Horse stallion, "Sun's Delight," a World Grand Champion.

Thoroughbred

Thoroughbred horses originated in England. The most common coat colors are bay, brown, black, or chestnut and, less frequently, roan or gray. White markings on the face and legs are common.

These horses are noted for their fineness of conformation and their long, straight, well-muscled legs. They are used as hunters and as saddle, stock, race, and polo horses.

Welsh Pony

Welsh Ponies originated in Wales. The coat may be any color except piebald or skewbald, but gaudy white markings are not popular.

FIGURE 25.—Thoroughbred stallion, "Buckpasser," winner of more than $1.4 million.

These ponies are an intermediate size between Shetland Ponies and other light horse breeds. The American Welsh Stud Book stipulates two height divisions: Division A cannot exceed 12–2 hands and Division B must be over 12–2 and not more than 14 hands.

Welsh Ponies are used for racing, trail riding, parading, stock cutting, and hunting, and as roadsters and mounts for children and small adults.

FIGURE 26.—Welsh Pony stallion, "1740 Liseter Shooting Star."

SELECTING AND JUDGING HORSES

Relatively few horses are inspected and evaluated by experienced judges. Most of them are bought by persons who lack experience in judging but who have a practical need for the animal and take pride in owning a good horse. Before buying a horse, an amateur should get the help of a competent horseman.

How to Select a Horse

When selecting a horse, the buyer must first decide what kind of horse he needs. This means that he must consider the following points.

(1) The mount should be purchased within a price range that the buyer can afford.

(2) The amateur or child should have a quiet, gentle, well-broken horse that is neither headstrong nor unmanageable. The horse should never be too spirited for the rider's skill.

(3) The size of the horse should be in keeping with the size and weight of the rider. A small child should have a small horse or pony, but a heavy man should have a horse of the weight-carrying type. Also, a tall man or woman looks out of place if not mounted on a horse of considerable height.

(4) Usually the novice will do best to start with a three-gaited horse and first master the three natural gaits before attempting to ride a horse executing the more complicated gaits.

(5) Other conditions being equal, the breed and color of horse may be decided on the basis of preference.

(6) The mount should be suited to the type of work to be performed.

After deciding on the kind of horse needed and getting an ideal in mind, the buyer is ready to select the individual horse. Selection on the basis of body conformation and performance is the best single method of obtaining a good horse. Of course, when animals are selected for breeding purposes, two additional criteria should be considered. These are (1) the record of the horse's progeny if the animal is old enough and has reproduced and (2) the animal's pedigree. Also, show-ring winnings may be helpful.

Proficiency in judging horses necessitates a knowledge of: (1) The parts of a horse, (2) the proper value assigned to each part (a score card may be used for this purpose), (3) blemishes and unsoundnesses, (4) ways to determine age, (5) the gaits, and (6) colors and markings.

Parts of a Horse

In selecting and judging horses, horsemen usually refer to parts rather than the individual as a whole. Nothing so quickly sets a real horseman apart from a novice as a thorough knowledge of the parts and the language commonly used in describing them. Figure 27 shows the parts of a horse.

Horse Score Card

A horse must conform to the specific type that is needed for the function he is to perform. Secondly, he should conform to the characteristics of the breed that he represents. The use of a score card is a good way to make sure that no part is overlooked and a proper value is assigned to each part.

A score card is a listing of the different parts of an animal, with a numerical value assigned to each part according to its relative importance. Also, breed characteristics may be considered in a score card. An all-breed horse score card is shown on page 13.

Blemishes and Unsoundnesses

An integral part of selecting a horse lies in the ability to recognize common blemishes and unsoundnesses and the ability to rate the importance of each.

A thorough knowledge of normal, sound structure makes it easy to recognize imperfections.

Any deviation from normal in the structure or function of a horse constitutes an unsoundness. From a practical standpoint, however, a differentiation is made between abnormalities that do and those that do not affect serviceability.

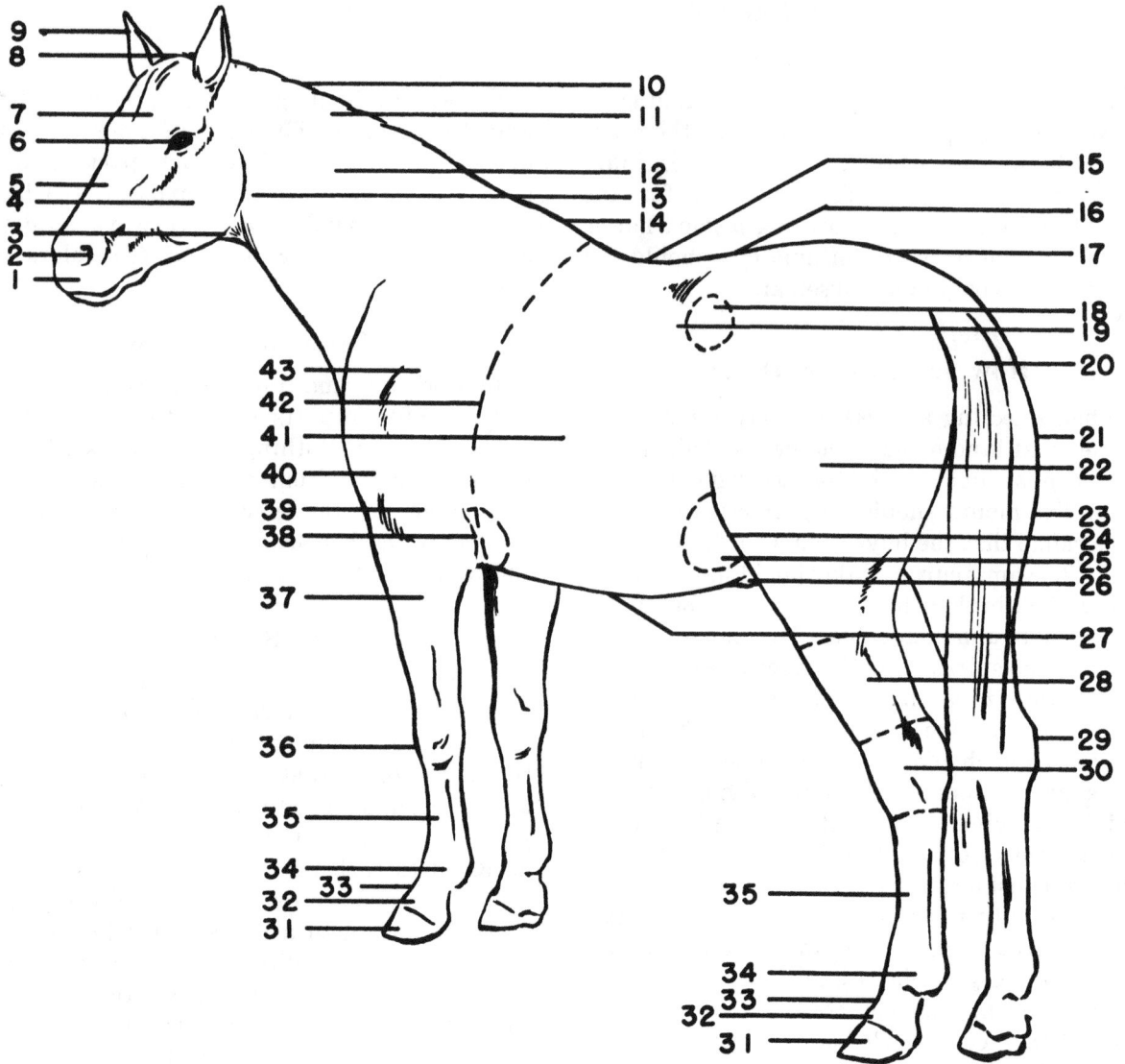

FIGURE 27.—Parts of a horse.

1. Muzzle	12. Neck	23. Quarter	34. Fetlock
2. Nostril	13. Throatlatch	24. Stifle	35. Cannon
3. Jaw	14. Withers	25. Rear flank	36. Knee
4. Cheek	15. Back	26. Sheath	37. Forearm
5. Face	16. Loin	27. Underline	38. Point of elbow
6. Eye	17. Croup	28. Gaskin	39. Arm
7. Forehead	18. Hip	29. Point of hock	40. Point of shoulder
8. Poll	19. Coupling	30. Hock	41. Ribs
9. Ear	20. Tail	31. Foot	42. Heart girth
10. Mane	21. Point of buttocks	32. Coronet	43. Shoulder
11. Crest	22. Thigh	33. Pastern	

BN–15178

ALL-BREED HORSE SCORE CARD

Characteristics	Points or percent	Name or number of horse:	Name or number of horse:	Name or number of horse:	Name or number of horse:
Breed type _____ Animals should possess the distinctive characteristics of the breed represented, including— *Color:* *Height at maturity:* *Weight at maturity:*	15				
Form _____ *Style and beauty:* Attractive, good carriage, alert, refined, symmetrical, and all parts nicely blended together. *Body:* Nicely turned; long well-sprung ribs; heavily muscled. *Back and loin:* Short and strong, wide, well muscled, and short coupled. *Croup:* Long, level, wide, muscular, with a high-set tail. *Rear quarters:* Deep and muscular. *Gaskin:* Heavily muscled. *Withers:* Prominent, and of the same height as the high point of the croup. *Shoulders:* Deep, well laid in, and sloping about a 45-degree angle. *Chest:* Fairly wide, deep, and full. *Arm and forearm:* Well muscled.	35				
Feet and legs _____ *Legs:* Correct position and set when viewed from front, side, and rear. *Pasterns:* Long, and sloping at about a 45-degree angle. *Feet:* In proportion to size of horse, good shape, wide and deep at heels, dense texture of hoof. *Hocks:* Deep, clean-cut, and well supported. *Knees:* Broad, tapered gradually into cannon. *Cannons:* Clean, flat, with tendons well defined.	15				
Head and neck _____ Alertly carried, showing style and character. *Head:* Well proportioned to rest of body, refined, clean-cut, with chiseled appearance; broad, full forehead with great width between the eyes; ears medium sized, well carried, and attractive; eyes large and prominent. *Neck:* Long, nicely arched, clean cut about the throatlatch, with head well set on, gracefully carried.	10				
Quality _____ Clean, flat bone; well-defined and clean joints and tendons, and fine skin and hair.	10				
Action _____ *Walk:* Easy, springy, prompt, balanced, a long step, with each foot carried forward in a straight line; feet lifted clear of the ground. *Trot:* Prompt, straight, elastic, balanced, with hocks carried closely, and high flection of knees and hocks.	15				
Discrimination: Any abnormality that affects the serviceability of the horse. *Disqualification:* In keeping with breed registry or show regulations.					
Total points or percent _____	100				

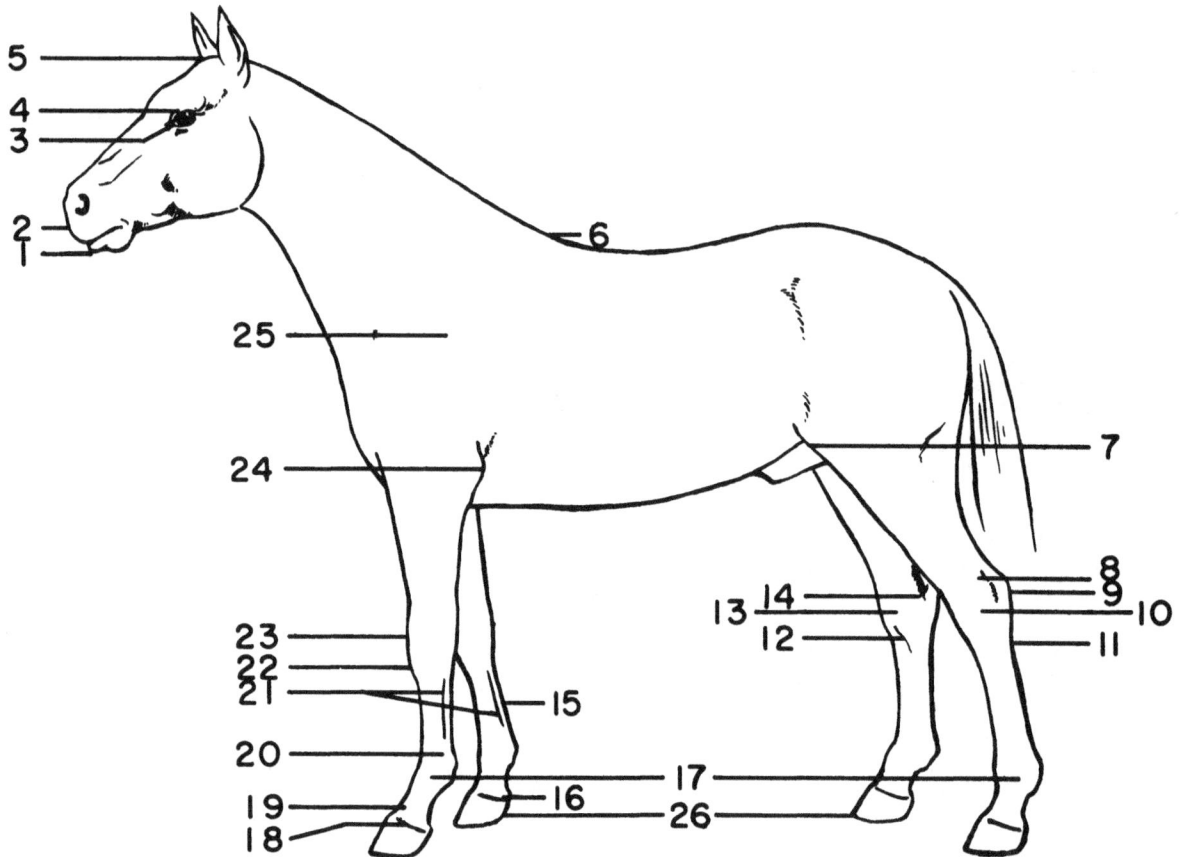

BN–15177

FIGURE 28.—Location of points of common unsoundnesses in horses.

1. Undershot jaw
2. Parrot mouth
3. Blindness
4. Moon blindness
5. Poll evil
6. Fistulous withers
7. Stifled
8. Thoroughpin

9. Capped hock
10. Stringhalt
11. Curb
12. Bone spavin or jack
13. Bog spavin
14. Blood spavin
15. Bowed tendons
16. Sidebones

17. Cocked ankles
18. Quittor
19. Ring bone
20. Windpuffs
21. Splints
22. Knee sprung
23. Calf kneed
24. Capped elbow

25. Sweeney
26. Contracted feet, corns, founder, thrush, quarter or sand crack, scratches or grease heel.

General: Heaves, hernia, thick wind, roaring.

Blemishes include abnormalities that do not affect serviceability, such as wire cuts, rope burns, nail scratches, or capped hocks.

Unsoundnesses include more serious abnormalities that affect serviceability.

Figure 28 shows the location of common blemishes and unsoundnesses.

A buyer should consider the use to which he intends to put the animal before he buys a blemished or unsound horse.

How to Determine Age

The lifespan of horses averages about 18 years. Horses generally are at their best between 3 and 12 years of age. This may vary because of individual differences in animals or because of differences in the kind of work they do.

The age of horses is, therefore, important to breeder, seller, and buyer.

TABLE 1.—*Types and number of teeth in horses*

Types of teeth	Number of teeth		
	Mature male	Mature female	Young animal, either sex
Molars or grinders _____	24	24	12
Incisors or front teeth __ ___ The 2 central incisors are known as centrals or nippers; the next 2, 1 on each side of the nippers, are called intermediates or middles; and the last, or outer pair, are the corners.	12	12	12
Tushes or pointed teeth ____ These are located between the incisors and molars in males. Females do not have tushes as a rule.	4	0	0
Total teeth _ ____ __ _____	40	36	24

The approximate age of a horse can be determined by noting time of appearance, shape, and degree of wear of temporary and permanent teeth. Temporary, or milk, teeth are easily distinguishable from permanent ones because they are smaller and whiter.

The best way to learn to determine age in horses is by examining the teeth of individual horses of known ages.

A mature male horse has 40 teeth and a mature female has 36, as shown in table 1.[6] A foal of either sex has 24. The mare does not have tushes as a rule.

Figures 29 to 43 are guides for determining the age of horses by their teeth.

Even experienced horsemen cannot determine the age of an animal accurately after it is

[6] Quite commonly, a small, pointed tooth, known as a "wolf tooth," may appear in front of each molar in the upper jaw, thus increasing the total number of teeth to 42 in the male and 38 in the female. Less frequently, two more wolf teeth in the lower jaw increase the total number of teeth in the male and female to 44 and 40, respectively.

12 years old. After this age, the teeth change from oval to triangular and they project or slant forward more and more as the horse becomes older.

Side views of the mouths of 5-, 7-, and 20-year-old horses are shown in figure 44.

An animal's environment can affect wear on the teeth. Teeth of horses raised in dry sandy areas, for example, will show more than normal wear; a 5-year-old western horse may have teeth that would be normal in a 6- to 8-year-old horse raised elsewhere. The teeth of cribbers also show more than normal wear. The age of such animals is hard to determine, and the age of horses with a parrot mouth also is difficult to estimate.

The Gaits

A gait is a particular way of going, either natural or acquired, that is characterized by a distinctive rhythmic movement of the feet and legs (fig. 45).

The walk is a natural, slow, flatfooted, four-beat gait. A four-beat gait is one in which each foot leaves and strikes the ground at separate intervals. The walk should be springy, regular, and true.

The trot is a natural, rapid, two-beat, diagonal gait in which a front foot and the opposite hind foot take off and strike the ground simultaneously. There is a brief moment when all four feet are off the ground and the horse seems to float through the air.

The canter is a slow, restrained, three-beat gait. Two diagonal legs are paired and produce a single beat that falls between the successive beats of the two unpaired legs. The canter imposes a special wear on the leading forefoot and its diagonal hindfoot. It is important, therefore, to change the lead frequently.

The lope is the western adaptation of a very slow canter. It is a smooth, slow gait in which the head is carried low.

The run or gallop is a fast, four-beat gait in which the feet strike the ground separately—first one hind foot, then the other hind foot, then the front foot on the same side as the first hind foot, and then the other front foot, which decides the lead. There is a brief interval when all four feet are off the ground. The gallop is the

16

FIGURE 29.—Temporary incisors to 10 days of age: First or central upper and lower temporary incisors appear.

FIGURE 30.—Temporary incisors at 4 to 6 weeks of age: Second or intermediate upper and lower temporary incisors appear.

FIGURE 31.—Temporary incisors at 6 to 10 months: Third or corner upper and lower temporary incisors appear.

FIGURE 32.—Temporary incisors at 1 year: Crowns of central temporary incisors show wear.

FIGURE 33.—Temporary incisors at 1½ years: Intermediate temporary incisors show wear.

FIGURE 34.—Temporary incisors at 2 years: All show wear.

FIGURE 35.—Incisors at 4 years: Permanent incisors replace temporary centrals and intermediates; temporary corner incisors remain.

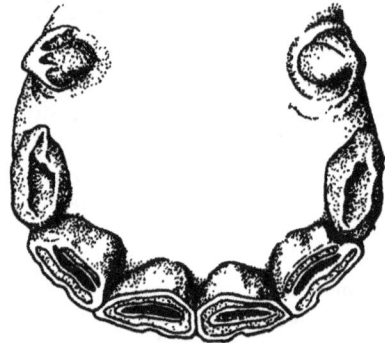

Figs. 29 to 36, BN–37807

FIGURE 36.—Incisors at 5 years: All permanent: cups in all incisors.

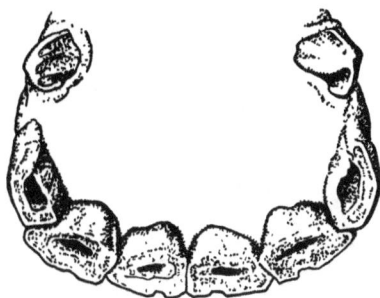

FIGURE 37.—Incisors at 6 years: Cups worn out of lower central incisors.

FIGURE 38.—Incisors at 7 years: Cups worn out of lower intermediate incisors.

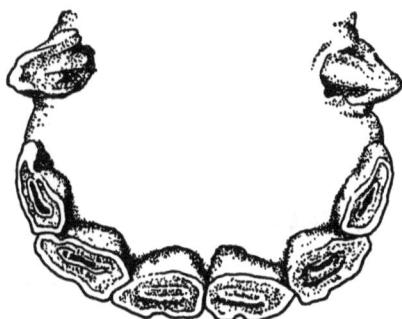

FIGURE 39.—Incisors at 8 years: Cups worn out of all lower incisors, and dental star (dark line in front of cup) appears on lower central and intermediate pairs.

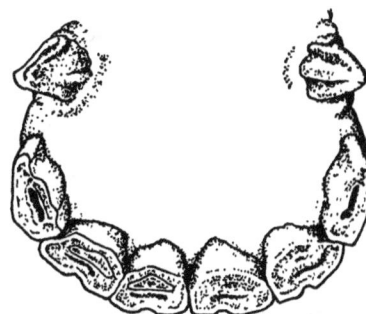

FIGURE 40.—Incisors at 9 years: Cups worn out of upper central incisors; dental star on upper central and intermediate pairs.

FIGURE 41.—Incisors at 10 years: Cups worn out of upper intermediate incisors, and dental star is present in all incisors.

FIGURE 42.—Incisors at 11 or 12 years: Cups worn in all incisors (smooth mouthed), and dental star approaches center of cups.

Figs. 37 to 43,
BN–37808

FIGURE 43.—Characteristic shape of lower incisors at 18 years.

18

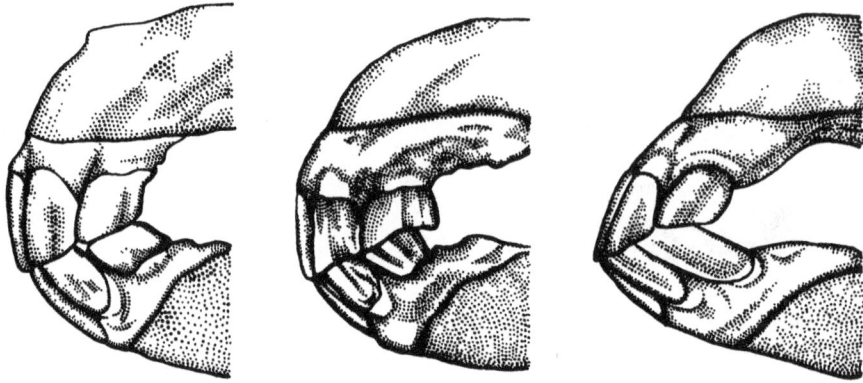

BN-5969

FIGURE 44.—Side view of 5-, 7-, and 20-year-old mouth. Note that as the horse advances in age, the teeth change from nearly perpendicular to slanting sharply toward the front.

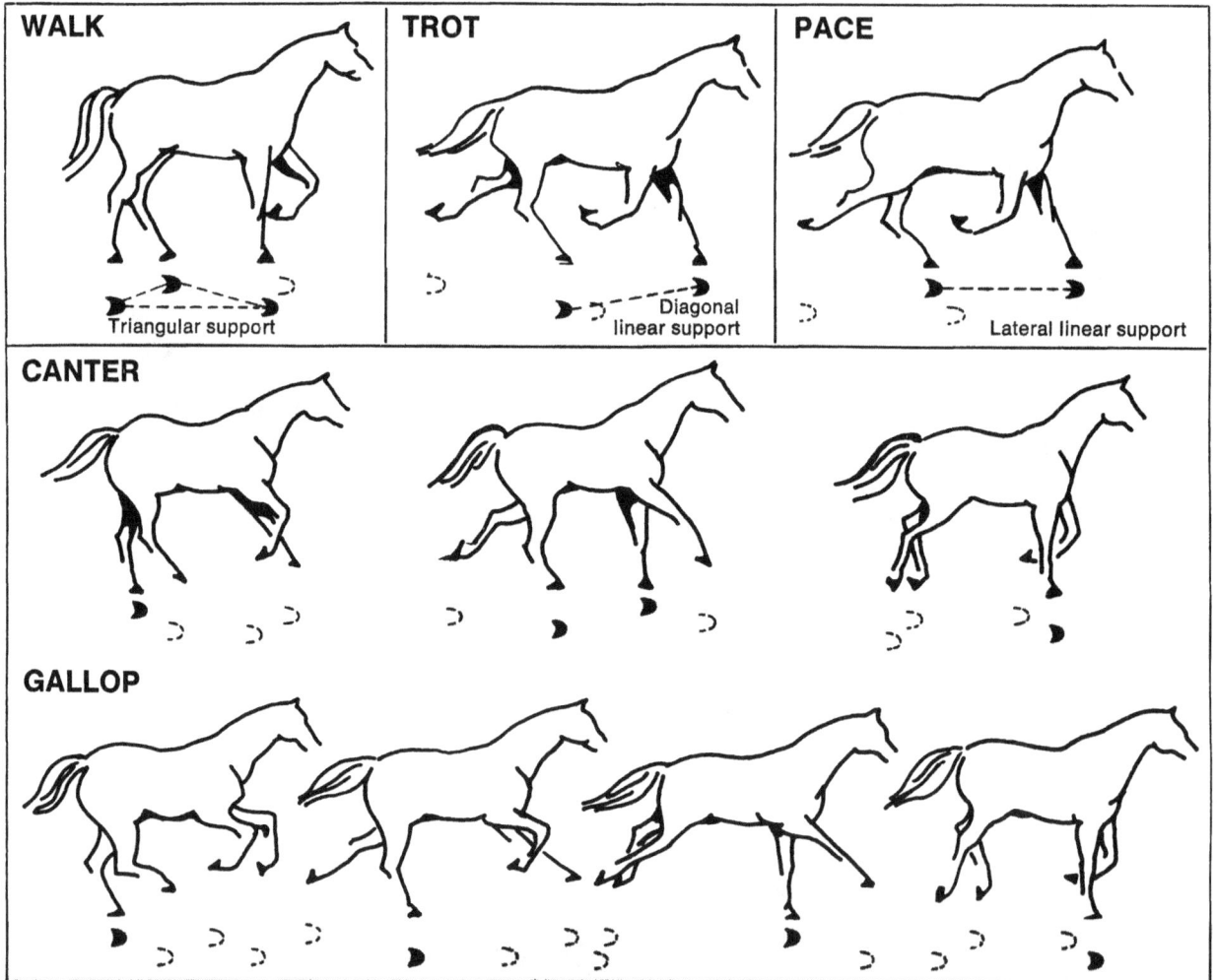

BN-37799

FIGURE 45.—The gaits of horses.

fast natural gait of both wild horses and Thoroughbred racehorses.

The pace is a fast two-beat gait in which the front and hind feet on the same side start and stop simultaneously. The feet rise just above the ground level. There is a split second when all four feet are off the ground and the horse seems to float through the air.

Colors and Markings of Horses

Within certain breeds, some colors are preferred or required, and others are undesirable or constitute disqualifications for registration.

A good horseman needs a working knowledge of horse colors and patterns because they are the most conspicuous features by which a horse can be described or identified.

Body colors

The five basic body colors of horses are as follows:

Bay.—Bay is a mixture of red and yellow. It includes many shades, from a light yellowish tan (light bay) to a dark, rich shade that is almost brown (dark bay). A bay horse usually has a black mane and tail and black points.

BN-37794

FIGURE 46.—The head marks of horses. Star is any white mark on the forehead located above a line running from eye to eye; stripe is a narrow white marking that extends from about the line of the eyes to the nostrils; blaze is a broad, white marking covering almost all the forehead but not including the eyes or nostrils; star, stripe, and snip includes all three of these marks; snip is a white mark between the nostrils or on the lips; bald is a bald, or white, face including the eyes and nostrils, or a partially white face; star and stripe incudes both a star and stripe.

Black.—A black horse is completely black, including the muzzle and flanks. If in doubt whether the horse is dark brown or black, note the color of the fine hairs on the muzzle and the hair on the flanks; tan or brown hairs at these points indicate the horse is not a true black, but a seal brown.

Brown.—A brown horse is almost black but can be distinguished by the fine tan or brown hairs on the muzzle or flanks.

Chestnut (sorrel).—A chestnut horse is basically red. The shades vary from light washy yellow (light chestnut) to a dark liver color (dark chestnut). Between these come the brilliant red-gold and copper shades. Normally, the mane and tail of a chestnut horse are the same shade as the body, although they may be lighter. When they are lighter, the coloring is called flaxen mane and tail. Chestnut color is never accompanied by a black mane and tail.

White.—A true white horse is born white and remains white throughout life. White horses have snow-white hair, pink skin, and brown eyes (rarely blue).

Besides the five basic colors, horses have five major variations to these coat colors. The variations are as follows:

Dun (buckskin).—Dun is a yellowish color of variable shading from pale yellow to a dirty canvas color. A dun horse has a stripe down the back.

Gray.—This is a mixture of white and black hairs. Sometimes a gray horse is difficult to distinguish from a black horse at birth, but gray horses get lighter with age.

Palomino.—This is a golden color. Palomino horses have a light colored mane and tail of white, silver, or ivory.

Pinto (calico or paint).—Pinto is a Spanish word that means painted. The pinto color is characterized by irregular colored and white areas in either piebald or skewbald patterns. Piebald horses are black and white, and skewbald horses are white and any other color except black.

Roan.—Roan is a mixture of white hairs with one or more base colors. White with bay is red roan; white with chestnut is strawberry roan; and white with black is blue roan.

Head marks

When identifying an individual horse, it is generally necessary to include more identification than just body color. For example, it may be necessary to identify the dark sorrel as the one with the blaze face. Some common head markings are shown in figure 46.

Leg marks

Leg marks are often used, along with head marks, to describe a horse. The most common leg marks are shown in figure 47.

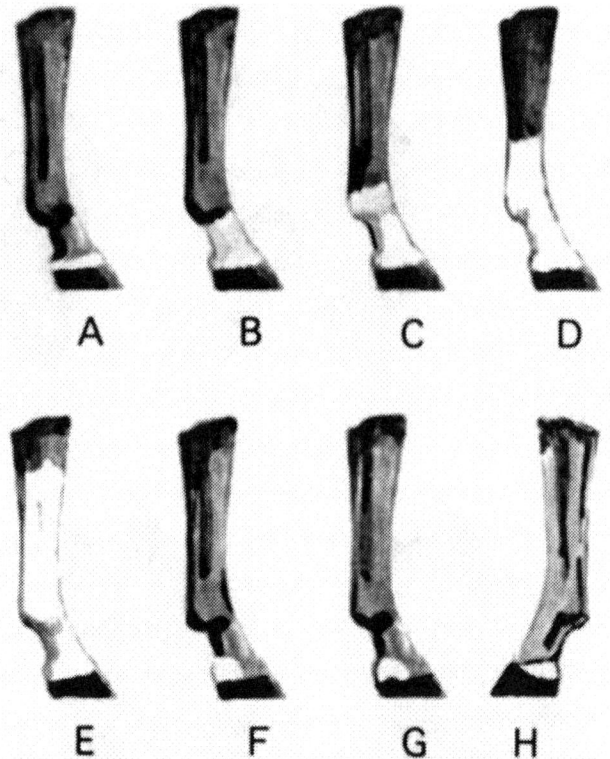

BN–37811

FIGURE 47.—The leg marks of horses. (A) Coronet, a white stripe covering the coronet band; (B) Pastern, white extends from the coronet to and including the pastern; (C) Ankle, white extends from the coronet to and including the fetlock; (D) Half stocking, white extends from the coronet to the middle of the cannon; (E) Stocking, white extends from the coronet to the knee, and when the white includes the knee the mark is called a full stocking; (F) White heels, both heels are white; (G) White outside heel, outside heel only is white; (H) White inside heel, inside heel only is white.

BREEDING HORSES

Horse owners who plan to breed one or more mares should have a working knowledge of heredity and know how to care for breeding animals and foals. The number of mares bred that actually conceive varies from about 40 to 85 percent, with the average running less than 50 percent. Some mares that do conceive fail to produce living foals. This means that, on the average, two mares are kept a whole year to produce one foal, and even then, some foals are disappointments from the standpoint of quality.

Heredity in Horses

The gene is the unit that determines heredity. In the body cells of horses there are many chromosomes. In turn, the chromosomes carry pairs of minute particles, called genes, which are the basic hereditary material (fig. 48). The nucleus of each body cell of horses contains 32 pairs of chromosomes, or a total of 64; whereas there are thousands of pairs of genes.

When a sex cell (a sperm or an egg) is formed, only one chromosome and one gene of each pair goes into it. Then, when mating and fertilization occur, the 32 single chromosomes from the germ cell of each parent unite to form new pairs, and the chromosomes with their

BN–37810

FIGURE 48.—A pair of bundles, called chromosomes, carrying minute particles, called genes. The genes determine all the hereditary characteristics of living animals, from length of leg to body size.

genes are again present in duplicate, in the body cells of the embryo. Thus, with all possible combinations of 32 pairs of chromosomes and the genes that they bear, it is not strange that full sisters (except identical twins from a single egg split after fertilization) are so different. Actually we can marvel that they bear as much resemblance to each other as they do.

Because of this situation, the mating of a mare with a fine track record to a stallion that transmits good performance characteristics will not always produce a foal of a merit equal to its parents. The foal could be markedly poorer than the parents or, in some cases, it could be better than either parent.

Simple and multiple gene inheritance occurs in horses, as in all animals. In simple gene inheritance, only one pair of genes is involved; thus, a pair of genes may be responsible for some one specific trait in horses. However, most characteristics, such as speed, are due to many genes; hence, they are called multiple-gene characteristics.

For most characteristics, many pairs of genes are involved. For example, growth rate in foals is affected by (1) appetite and feed consumption, (2) the proportion of the feed eaten that is absorbed, and (3) the use to which the nutrients are put—whether they are used for growth or fattening, and each in turn is probably affected by different genes. Because multiple characteristics show all manner of gradation from high to low performance, they are sometimes referred to as quantitative traits. Thus, quantitative inheritance refers to the degree to which a characteristic is inherited. For example, all racehorses can run and all inherit some ability to run, but it is the degree to which they inherit the ability that is important.

Dominant and recessive factors exist in horses. Some genes have the ability to prevent or mask the expression of others, with the result that the genetic makeup of such animals cannot be recognized with accuracy. This is called dominance. The gene that is masked is recessive. Because black is dominant to chestnut, all of the offspring will be black when a

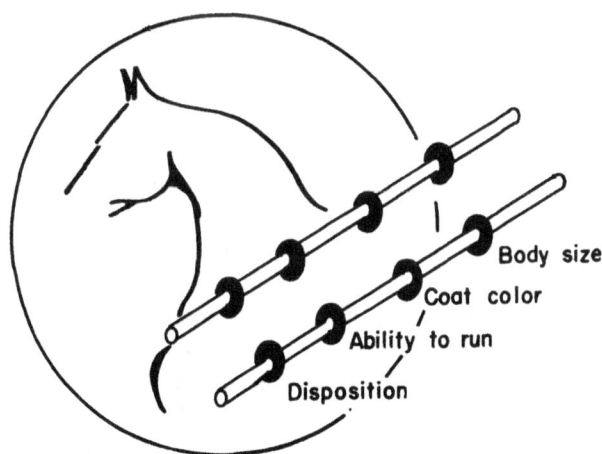

22

pure black stallion is crossed with a chestnut mare.

The resulting black offspring are not genotypically pure; they are Bb, where B stands for the dominant black and b for the recessive chestnut. These black, or F_1 (first cross), animals will produce germ cells carrying black and chestnut genes in equal proportion (fig. 49). Then if an F_1 stallion is crossed with F_1 mares, the F_2 (second cross) population will on the average consist of three blacks to one chestnut.

The chestnut in the F_2 population, being a recessive, will be pure for color. That is, the mating of any two chestnut horses will produce, according to the most authoritative work, chestnut offspring; this is the situation in the Suffolk breed of draft horses where all animals of the breed are chestnuts. Of the three

blacks in the F_2, however, only one is pure for black with the genetic constitution BB. The other two will be Bb in genetic constitution and will produce germ cells carrying B and b in equal proportion.

Dominance often makes it difficult to identify and discard all animals carrying an undesirable recessive factor. In some cases, dominance is neither complete nor absent, but incomplete, or partial, and expressed in a variety of ways. The best known case of partial dominance in horses is the palomino coloring.

Heredity and environment in quantitative traits function in horses just as they do in all animals. Therefore, maximum development of characteristics of economic importance such as growth, body form, or speed cannot be achieved unless horses receive proper training, nutrition, and management.

The problem of the horse breeder is to select the best animals available genetically to be parents of the next generation. Because only 15 to 30 percent of the observed variation among animals may be due to heredity, and because environmental differences can produce misleading variations, mistakes in the selection of breeding animals are inevitable.

The sex of an animal is determined by chromosomes. The mare has a pair of similar chromosomes called X chromosomes, and the stallion has a pair of unlike sex chromosomes called X and Y chromosomes.

The sex chromosomes in each pair separate from one another when the germ cells are formed. Thus, each of the ova or eggs produced by the mare contains the X chromosome; but the sperm of the stallion are of two types, one-half containing the X chromosome and the other half the Y chromosome (fig. 50). Since, on the average, the eggs and sperm unite at random, it can be understood that half of the progeny will contain the chromosomal makeup XX (female) and other half XY (male).

Both the stallion and the mare are equally important to any one offspring. But a stallion generally can have many more offspring than a mare can and, from a hereditary standpoint, is more important to the herd or breed.

Prepotency is the ability of an animal to stamp its characteristics on its offspring so the

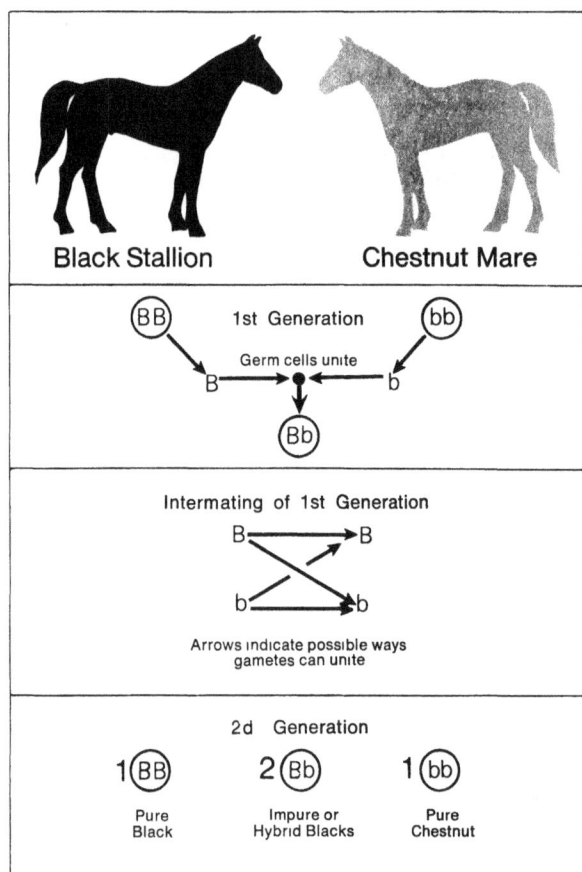

BN–37806

FIGURE 49.—Gene inheritance in horses.

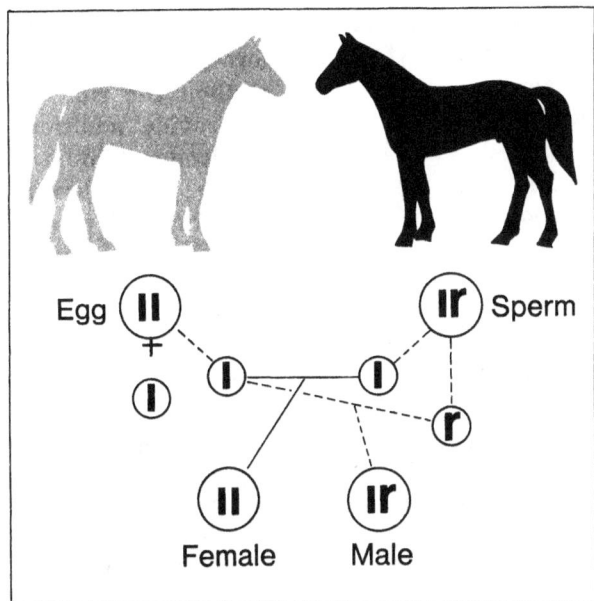

FIGURE 50.—An illustration of the mechanism of sex determination in horses, showing how sex is determined by the chromosomal makeup of the individual.

offspring resemble that parent or they resemble each other more than usual.

Nicking results when the right combination of genes for good characteristics is contributed by each parent. Thus, animals nick well when their respective combinations of good genes complement each other.

Family names of horses have genetic significance only if (1) they are based on a linebreeding program that keeps the family closely related to the admired stallion or mare carrying the particular name and (2) members of the family have been rigidly culled. Family names, therefore, lend themselves to speculation, and often have no more significance than human family names.

Systems of breeding, whether planned or by chance, have made it possible to produce horses specially adapted to riding, racing, or driving. There is no one best system of breeding or secret of success for all conditions. Each breeding program is an individual case, requiring careful study. The choice of the system of breeding should be determined primarily by the size and quality of the herd, by the finances and skill of the operator, and by the ultimate goal ahead.

The systems of breeding from which the horseman may select are discussed as follows:

(1) Purebreeding is the system in which the lineage, regardless of the number of generations removed, traces back to the foundation animals accepted by the breed or to animals that have been subsequently approved for infusion. Purebreeding may be conducted as either inbreeding or outcrossing, or part of each.

(2) Inbreeding is the mating of animals more closely related than the average of the population from which they came. It may be done either by closebreeding or linebreeding.

(a) Closebreeding is breeding closely related animals such as sire to daughter, son to dam, or brother to sister.

(b) Linebreeding is breeding related animals so as to keep the offspring closely related to some highly admired ancestor such as half brother to half sister, female descendent to grandsire, or cousin to cousin.

(3) Outcrossing is the mating of animals that are members of the same breed but that show no relationship in the pedigree for at least four to six generations.

(4) Grading up is breeding a purebred sire of a given breed to a native, or grade, female.

(5) Crossbreeding is mating animals of different breeds.

The Stallion

The stallion should be a purebred animal, a good representative of the breed selected, and a superior individual in type and soundness. If he is an older horse with progeny, the progeny should be of uniformly high quality and of approved type and soundness.

Reproductive organs of the stallion

The stallion's functions in reproduction are (1) to produce the male reproductive cells, the sperm, or spermatozoa, and (2) to introduce sperm into the female reproductive tract at the proper time. Figure 51 is a schematic drawing of the reproductive organs of the stallion.

The two testicles are the primary sex organs of the stallion. They produce the sperm and a

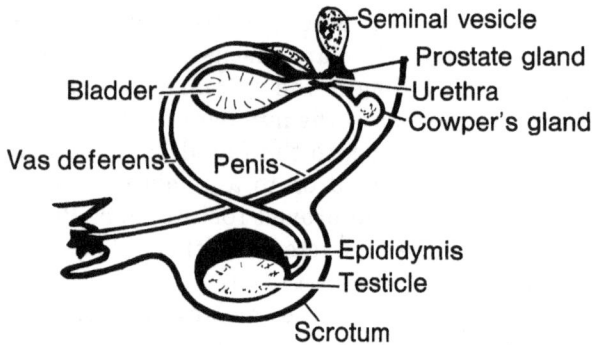

FIGURE 51.—Reproductive organs of the stallion.

hormone called testosterone, which regulates and maintains the male reproductive tract in its functional state and is responsible for the masculine appearance and behavior of the stallion.

Sperm are produced in the inner walls or surface of the seminiferous tubules, which are a mass of minute, coiled tubules. These tubules merge into a series of larger ducts that carry the sperm to a coiled tube called the epididymis. The epididymis is the place where the sperm are stored and where they mature, or ripen.

The testicles and epididymides are enclosed in the scrotum, the chief function of which is thermoregulatory. The scrotum maintains the testicles at temperatures several degrees cooler than the rest of the body.

From the epididymis, the sperm move through a tube, the vas deferens, into the urethra. The urethra has a dual role. It carries urine from the bladder through the penis and sperm from the junction with the vas deferens to the end of the penis.

Along the urethra are the accessory glands. These are the prostate, the seminal vesicles, and cowper's gland. Their fluids nourish and preserve the sperm and provide a medium that transports the sperm. The fluids and sperm combined are called semen.

Care and management of the stallion

The following points are pertinent to the care and management of the stallion.

Quarters.—The most convenient arrangement is a roomy box stall that opens directly into a 2- or 3-acre pasture.

Feeding.—The feed requirements are covered in the section on feeding horses.

Exercise.—Allow the stallion the run of a sizeable pasture but also provide additional, unhurried exercise either under saddle or hitched to a cart; by longeing; or by leading.

Grooming.—Groom the stallion daily to make him more attractive and to assist in maintaining his good health and condition.

Age and service.—Limit the mature stallion to not more than two services per day, one early in the morning and the other late in the afternoon; allow 1 day of rest each week.

The number of hand matings per year for stallions of different ages should be limited as follows: 2 years old, 10 to 15; 3 years old, 20 to 40; 4 years old, 30 to 60; mature horses, 80 to 100; and over 18 years old, 20 to 40. Limit the 2-year-olds to two to three services per week; the 3-year-olds to one service per day; and the 4-year-olds or over to two services per day. A stallion may remain a vigorous and reliable breeder up to 20 to 25 years of age.

There are breed differences. Thus, when first entering stud duty, the average 3-year-old Thoroughbred should be limited to 20 to 25 mares per season, but a Standardbred of the same age may breed 25 to 30 mares. A 4- to 5-year-old Thoroughbred should be limited to 30 to 40 mares per season, but a Standardbred of the same age may breed 40 to 50 mares.

Stallion Breeding Contract

The stallion breeding contract should always be in writing; and the higher the stud fee, the more important it is that good business methods are practiced. Neither "gentlemen's agreements" nor "barn door records" will suffice.

A breeding contract is binding on the parties who sign it. Thus, the contract should be carefully read and fully understood before it is signed.

A sample stallion breeding contract is shown on page 25. The contract should be executed in duplicate for each mare, one copy to be retained by each party.

The Mare

Characteristics found in the broodmare are likely to be reflected in the offspring. It is fun-

Breeding Contract

This contract for the breeding season of _____ made and entered into by and between _____ ,
(year) (owner of stallion)

_____ , herein after designated stallion owner, and _____ , _____ ,
(address) (owner of mare) (address)

hereinafter designated mare owner.

This contract covers—

The stallion, _____ , whose service fee is $ _____ ; $ _____ of which is paid
(name of stallion)

with this contract and the balance will be paid before the mare leaves _____ .
(name of farm or ranch)

and

The mare, _____ , reg. no. _____ , by _____ out of _____ ,
(name of mare) (sire) (dam)

age _____ , color_____ .

The mare owner agrees that—

Upon arrival, the mare will (a) be halter broken, (b) have the hind shoes removed, and (c) be accompanied by a health certificate signed by a veterinarian, certifying that she is healthy and in sound breeding condition.

Stallion owner will not be responsible for accident, disease, or death to the mare, or to her foal (if she has a foal).

Stallion owner may, at his discretion, have his veterinarian (a) check and treat the mare for breeding condition or diseases, and (b) treat her for parasites if needed, with the expenses of such services charged to the mare owner's account and paid when the mare leaves the farm or ranch.

He will pay the following board on his mare at the time the mare leaves the farm or ranch: Feed and facilities $ _____ per day.

Should the mare prove barren, or should the foal die at birth, he will send notice of same, signed by a licensed veterinarian, within 5 days of such barren determination or death.

Should he fail to deliver the above mare to the stallion owner's premises on or before _____ , stallion
(date)

owner shall be under no further obligation with respect to any matter herein set forth.

This contract shall not be assigned or transferred. In the event the mare is sold, any remaining unpaid fee shall immediately become due and payable and no refund shall be due anyone under any circumstances.

The stallion owner agrees that—

He will provide suitable facilities for the mare and feed and care for her in a good and husbandlike manner.

Mare owner will not be responsible for any disease, accident, or injury to stallion owner's horses.

A live foal is guaranteed—meaning a foal that can stand up alone and nurse.

The stallion owner and mare owner mutually agree that—

This contract is not valid unless completed in full.

Should the above named stallion die or become unfit for service, or should the above named mare die or become unfit to breed, this contract shall become null and void and money paid as part of this contract shall be refunded to mare owner.

Should the mare prove barren, or should the foal die at birth, with certification of same provided to stallion owner within the time specified, the stallion owner has the option either to (a) rebreed the mare the following year, or (b) refund the $ _____ portion of the breeding fee, thereby cancelling this entire contract.

The mare will not receive more than _____ covers during the breeding season, and she will not be
(number)

bred before _____ , 19___ , or after _____ , 19___ .

_____   _____   _____
(date) (signature, mare owner or rep.) (address)

_____   _____   _____
(date) (signature, stallion owner or rep.) (address)

damental that "like tends to produce like." The broodmare should possess an abundance of femininity in addition to being sound and of good type. She should be of good ancestry, whether purebred or grade.

Reproductive organs of the mare

The mare's functions in reproduction are to (1) produce the female reproductive cells, the eggs or ova; (2) develop the new individual, the embryo, in the uterus; (3) expel the fully developed young at the time of birth, or parturition; and (4) produce milk for the nourishment of the young.

The part played by the mare in the generative process is much more complicated than that of the stallion. It is imperative, therefore, that the modern horseman have a full understanding of the anatomy of the reproductive organs of the mare and the functions of each part. Figure 52 shows the reproductive organs of the mare.

The two ovaries are the primary sex organs of the mare. They are somewhat bean-shaped organs 2 to 3 inches long. The ovaries produce eggs. Each egg is contained in a bubblelike sac on the ovary, called a follicle. There are hundreds of follicles on each ovary. Generally, the follicles remain unchanged until puberty when one of them begins to grow because of an increase in the follicular liquid in it; the others remain small. The egg is suspended in the follicular fluid.

When the growing follicle is about an inch in diameter, a hormone causes it to rupture and discharge the egg. This is known as ovulation and is the time when mating should take place. The egg is trapped in a funnel-shaped membrane, called the infundibulum, that surrounds the ovary. The infundibulum narrows into a tube called the oviduct. The oviduct then carries the egg to the uterus, or womb, the largest of the female reproductive organs, where the unborn young, or fetus, will develop.

The lining of the uterus is soft and spongy. It contains a vast network of blood vessels that provide a "bed" for the fertilized egg to settle into and develop. At birth, the heavy layers of muscles of the uterus wall contract with great pressure to force the new animal out through the cervix and vagina.

Breeding habits and care of the mare

A knowledge of the mare's normal breeding habits will help to improve the fertility rate. However, not all mares that conceive give birth to live foals. So, improved care and management of the pregnant mare are important also. The age of puberty for mares is 12 to 15 months; the duration of heat ranges from 1 to 37 days, and averages 4 to 6 days; the interval between heat periods ranges from 10 to 37 days, and averages 21; and the gestation period ranges from 310 to 370 days, and averages 336.

The following points are pertinent to the care and management of the mare:

Age to breed.—Well-grown fillies may be bred as 2-year-olds, but most fillies are not bred until they are 3 years old.

Normal breeding season and time of foaling. —Spring is the ideal season for both breeding and foaling. Persons who race or show horses want foals to be born as soon as possible after January 1.

Conditioning for breeding.—Mares are conditioned by proper feeding and adequate exercise.

Signs of heat.—In season, mares generally exhibit (1) relaxation of the external genitals, (2) more frequent urination, (3) teasing of the other mares, (4) apparent desire for company, and (5) slight mucus discharge from the vagina.

The breeding operation.—No phase of horse production has become more unnatural or more complicated with domestication than the actual

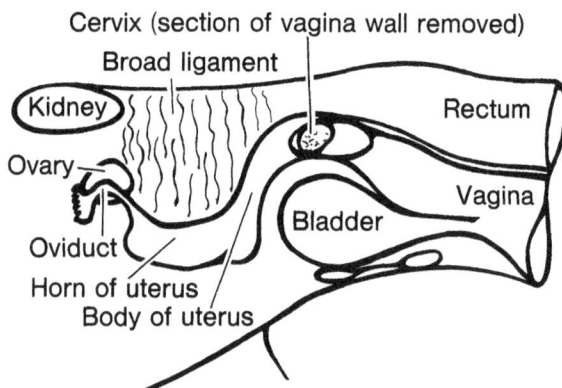

Cervix (section of vagina wall removed)
Broad ligament
Kidney
Rectum
Ovary
Vagina
Bladder
Oviduct
Horn of uterus
Body of uterus

BN–37804

FIGURE 52.—Reproductive organs of the mare.

breeding operation. This is so because breeders try to get mares bred in about 4 months instead of 12 and have arbitrarily limited the breeding season to late winter and early spring. The following facts and pointers are pertinent to the breeding operation:

(1) Hand mating, in which the animals are coupled under supervision, is the most common. It guards against injury to both the stallion and the mare. However, corral or pasture breeding may be preferable under certain conditions. For example, corral breeding may be resorted to when only one person is handling the breeding operation, and pasture breeding is sometimes followed on the ranges of the West. In corral breeding, the stallion and the mare are turned together in a corral; in pasture breeding, the stallion is turned to pasture with a band of mares.

(2) Breed only healthy mares to a healthy stallion. Require that all mares from the outside be accompanied by a health certificate signed by a veterinarian.

(3) Teasing is the best way in which to make certain that a mare is in season.

(4) Serve the mare daily or every other day during the heat period, beginning with the third day.

(5) After making certain that the mare is in season, wash the reproductive organs of the stallion and the external parts of the mare that are likely to come in contact with the reproductive organs of the stallion; bandage the upper 6 to 8 inches of the mare's tail. Place a twitch and hobbles on the mare and allow the sexual act to be completed. Return the mare for retrial approximately 21 days later.

Signs and tests of pregnancy.—The signs of pregnancy are (1) cessation of the heat period and (2) observed movement of the fetus through the abdominal walls. A veterinarian or an experienced horseman can determine pregnancy by making a rectal examination 40 to 60 days after the last service. Also, tests can be made by a laboratory.

Quarters for the pregnant mare.—Pregnant, idle mares should be turned to pasture. Pregnant mares that are used under saddle or in harness may be given quarters like those of other horses used similarly.

Feeding the pregnant mare.—Nutritive requirements are discussed in the feeding section of this handbook.

Exercise.—Mares that have the run of a large pasture will usually get sufficient exercise. Stabled mares should be exercised moderately for an hour daily under saddle or hitched to a cart. Continue this routine to within a day or two of foaling. During the last couple of days, mares may be led.

Signs of approaching parturition.—These signs are a distended udder, which may be observed 2 to 6 weeks before foaling; a shrinkage or falling away of the buttocks muscles near the tailhead and a falling of the abdomen 7 to 10 days before foaling; filling out of the teats 4 to 6 days before foaling; and the appearance of wax on the ends of the nipples 4 to 6 days before foaling. As foaling time draws nearer, the vulva becomes full and loose; milk drops from the teats; and the mare becomes restless, may break into a sweat, urinates frequently, and lies down and gets up. But there are times when all signs fail, so be prepared 30 days in advance of the expected time.

Foaling place.—When the weather is warm and it can be arranged, allow the mare to foal in a clean pasture away from other livestock. During bad weather, use a box stall which has been cleaned and disinfected with 13 ounces of lye in 10 gallons of water; use one-half strength solution in scrubbing mangers and grain boxes. Sprinkle the floor and walls lightly with quick lime or burnt lime. Provide plenty of bedding for the occasion.

Foaling time.—The following information and procedure may be helpful during foaling:

(1) The feed should be decreased and wheat bran should be added.

(2) An attendant should be near but not in sight.

(3) Normal presentation consists in the front feet coming first with the heels down (fig. 53). If there is any other presentation, a veterinarian should be summoned at once.

(4) Make certain that the newborn foal is breathing and that the membrane has been removed from its mouth and nostrils. Then rub and dry the foal with towels, treat the navel cord with tincture of iodine, and let the mare

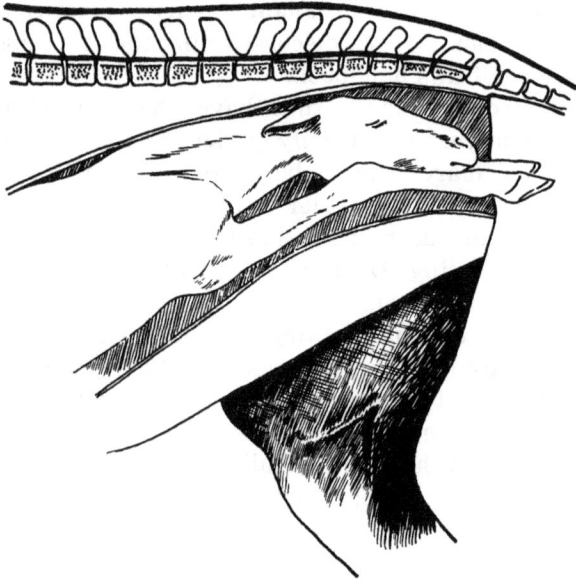

BN–33854

FIGURE 53.—Normal presentation. The back of the fetus is directly toward that of the mother, the forelegs are extended toward the vulva with the heels down, and the nose rests between the forelegs.

and foal rest for a time. Remove the expelled afterbirth from the stall and burn or bury it; it is usually expelled within 1 to 6 hours after foaling. Clean and rebed the stall after the mare and foal are up. Give the mare small quantities of lukewarm water at intervals and feed considerable wheat bran for the first few days after foaling; take 7 to 10 days to get the mare on full feed. Be observant; if the mare has much temperature, call a veterinarian. The normal temperature is 100.5° F.

Breeding after foaling.—Some horsemen rebreed mares during the first heat after foaling, usually on the 8th or 9th day, providing the birth was normal and the mare suffered no injury or infection. Other horsemen prefer to rebreed mares during the heat period that follows the foal heat (25 to 30 days from foaling), provided there is no discharge or evidence of infection.

The Foal

After the newborn foal starts breathing and has been rubbed dry, put it in one corner of the stall on clean, fresh straw. The mare usually will be less restless if this corner is in the direction of her head.

Protect the eyes of a newborn foal from bright lights.

Treatment of the navel cord

If left alone, the navel cord of the newborn foal usually breaks within 2 to 4 inches of the belly. If it does not break, cut it about 2 inches from the belly with clean dull shears or scrape it in two with a knife. A torn or broken blood vessel will bleed very little, but one cut directly across may bleed excessively. Treat the severed cord immediately with tincture of iodine, or other reliable antiseptic; then leave the mare and foal alone so they can rest and gain strength.

Value of colostrum

Colostrum is milk secreted by the dam for the first few days after parturition. It differs from ordinary milk in that it is more concentrated; is higher in protein content, especially in globulin; is richer in vitamin A; contains antibodies that protect the foal temporarily against certain infections; and is a natural purgative that removes fecal matter accumulated in the digestive tract.

Do not dissipate the benefits of colostrum by "milking out" a mare shortly before foaling time.

The first nursing

A strong, healthy foal will be on its feet and ready to nurse within $1/2$ to 2 hours after birth. Before allowing the foal to nurse for the first time, wash the mare's udder with a mild disinfectant and rinse thoroughly with clean, warm water.

A big, awkward foal occasionally needs assistance and guidance when it nurses the first time. If the foal is stubborn, forced feeding will be useless. Back the mare onto additional bedding in one corner of the stall and coax the foal to the teats with a bottle and nipple. An attendant may hold the bottle while standing on the opposite side of the mare from the foal.

A very weak foal should be given the mare's first milk even if it is necessary to draw this milk into a bottle and feed the foal one or two times by nipple. An attendant sometimes must steady a foal before it will nurse.

Bowel movement

Regulation of the bowel movement of the foal is very important. Constipation and diarrhea (scours) are common ailments.

Excrement impacted in the bowels during prenatal development—material called meconium—may kill the foal if it is not eliminated promptly. A good feed of colostrum usually will cause natural elimination. This is not always the case, however, especially when foals are from stall-fed mares.

Observe the foal's bowel movement 4 to 12 hours after birth. If there has been no fecal discharge by this time, and the foal seems sluggish and fails to nurse, give it an enema. Use 1 to 2 quarts of water at body heat (101° F.) mixed with a little glycerin, or use 1 to 2 quarts of warm, soapy water. Inject the solution with a baby syringe that has about a 3-inch nipple, or use a tube and can. Repeat the treatment until normal yellow feces appear.

If the foal is scouring, reduce the mare's feed and take away part of her milk from the foal at intervals by milking her out.

Diarrhea or scours in foals may result from infectious diseases or dirty surroundings. It is caused by an irritant in the digestive tract that should be removed. Give an astringent only in exceptional cases and on the advice of a veterinarian.

Conditions that may cause diarrhea are contaminated udder or teats, nonremoval of fecal matter from the digestive tract, fretfulness or temperature above normal in the mare, too much feed affecting the quality of the mare's milk, a cold damp bed, or continued exposure to cold rains.

Care of the suckling foal

Weather conditions permitting, there is no better place for a mare and foal than on pasture. When the foal is from 10 days to 3 weeks old, it will begin to nibble on a little grain and hay. To promote thrift and early development, and to avoid any setback at weaning time, encourage the foal to eat supplementary feed as early as possible (fig. 54). The foal should be provided with a low-built grain box especially

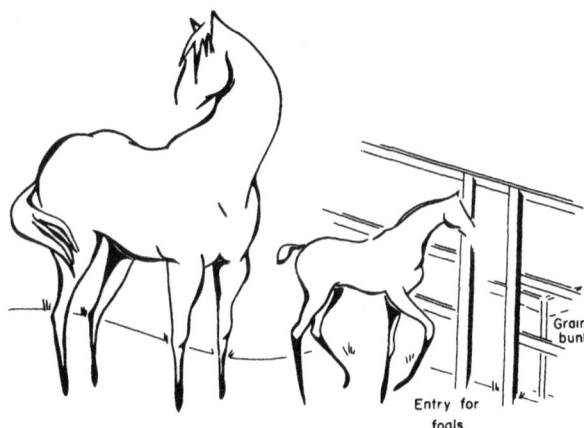

BN–33851

FIGURE 54.—A foal creep. With this arrangement, the foal can be fed separately from the dam.

for this purpose, or, if on pasture, the foal may be creep fed.

Rolled oats and wheat bran, to which a little brown sugar has been added, is especially palatable as a starting ration. Crushed or ground oats, cracked or ground corn, wheat bran, and a little linseed meal may be provided later with good results. Or a good commercial ration may be fed if desired and available.

Give the foal good hay, preferably a legume, or pasture in addition to its grain ration. A normal healthy foal should be eating one-half pound of grain daily per 100 pounds of body weight at 4 to 5 weeks of age. This ration should be increased by weaning time to about three-fourths of a pound or more per 100 pounds of body weight. The exact amount of the ration varies with the individual, the type of feed, and the development desired.

Foals normally reach one-half of their mature weight during the first year under such a system. Most breeders of Thoroughbreds and Standardbreds plan to have their 2-year-old animals at full height. Such results require liberal feeding from the beginning. A foal stunted in the first year by insufficient feeding cannot be developed properly later in life. It is well recognized that forced development must be done expertly if the animals are to remain durable and sound.

Training the foal

If the foal is trained early, it will be a better disciplined, more serviceable horse. Give lessons to the foal one at a time and in proper sequence; that is, be sure the pupil masters one lesson before it is given the next one.

Put a well-fitted halter on the foal when it is 10 to 14 days old. When the foal has become accustomed to the halter, in a day or so, tie the foal securely in the stall beside the mare. Try to keep the foal from freeing itself from the rope or from becoming tangled up in it.

Leave the foal tied 30 to 60 minutes each day for 2 or 3 days. Groom the animal carefully while it is tied. Rub each leg and handle each foot so that the foal becomes accustomed to having its feet picked up. After the foal has been groomed, lead it around with the mare for a few days and then lead it by itself. Lead it at both the walk and the trot. Many breeders of Thoroughbreds teach a foal to lead simply by leading it with the mare from the stall to the paddock and back again.

At this stage of the training, be sure the foal executes your commands to stop and go as soon as you give them. When halted, make the foal stand in show position—squarely on all four legs with its head up.

Use all your patience, gentleness, and firmness in training the foal. Never let your temper get the best of you.

Weaning

Foals usually are weaned at 4 to 6 months of age. Thorough preparation facilitates weaning.

It may be advisable to wean the foal at a comparatively early age if either the foal or mare is not doing well, if the mare is being given heavy work, or if the mare was rebred on the ninth day after foaling.

If by using a creep or a separate grain box the foal has become accustomed to eating a considerable amount of hay and about three-fourths of a pound of grain daily per 100 pounds of body weight, weaning will cause only a slight disturbance or setback. If the ration of the dam is cut in half a few days before the separation, her udder usually will dry up without difficulty.

Move the mare to new quarters from the stall she shares with the foal. Remove anything in the stall on which the foal might hurt itself during the first unhappy days that it lives alone. Make the separation of the foal from the mare complete and final. If the foal sees, hears, or smells its dam again, the separation process must be started all over again.

Decrease the mare's ration before and during weaning. Rub camphorated oil or a mixture of lard and spirits of camphor on the udder, but do not milk out the udder until 5 to 7 days later when it is soft and flabby.

Turn the foal out on pasture after a day or two. If there are several weanlings together, some of them might get hurt while running and frolicking in the pasture. Guard against this by first turning out two or three less valuable individuals and letting them tire themselves; then turn out the rest.

At this stage, if numerous weanlings are involved, separate them by sexes. Put the more timid ones by themselves. Do not run weanlings with older horses.

Castration

Geldings, or castrated males, are safer and easier to handle than stallions. Therefore, a colt should be castrated unless he is to be saved for breeding purposes. Have a veterinarian perform this operation. A colt may be castrated when only a few days old, but most horsemen prefer to delay the operation until the animal is about a year old. While there is less real danger to the animal and much less setback with early altering, it results in imperfect development of the foreparts. Delaying castration for a time results in more muscular, bolder features and better carriage of the foreparts.

Weather and management conditions permitting, the time of altering should be determined by the development of the individual. Underdeveloped colts may be left uncastrated 6 months or even a year longer than overdeveloped ones.

Breeders of Thoroughbred horses usually prefer to race them first as uncastrated animals.

There is less danger of infection if colts are castrated in the spring soon after they are turned out on clean pasture and before hot weather and "fly time" arrive. This is extremely important in the Southern States because of the danger of screwworm infestation.

Breaking

A foal will not need breaking if it has been trained properly. When a young horse can be saddled or harnessed with satisfactory ease, it is because the suggested training program has been followed. Saddling and harnessing are just additional steps. A good time to harness and work the horse for the first time is during the winter as a rising 2-year-old.

Raising the orphan foal

Occasionally, a mare dies during or immediately after parturition, leaving an orphan foal to be raised. At other times, a mare may fail to give sufficient milk, or she may have twins. In such cases, the foal may be (1) shifted to another mare, known as a foster mother or nurse mare, or (2) placed on mare's milk replacer, or synthetic milk, that is mixed and fed according to the manufacturer's directions.

It is important, however, that the orphan foal receive colostrum, preferably for about the first 4 days of life. For this purpose, colostrum from a mare that produces excess milk or one that has lost her foal should be collected and frozen from time to time; then, as needed, it may be thawed and warmed to 100° to 105° F. and fed.

For the first few days, the orphan foal should be fed with a bottle and rubber nipple. Within about 2 weeks, it may be taught to drink from a pail. All receptacles must be kept sanitary (clean and scald each time they are used) and feeding must be at regular intervals. Dry feeding should be started at the earliest possible time with the orphan foal.

The following formula may be used for feeding the orphan foal if a substitute milk must be used:

1 pint of low fat cow's milk (2% fat).
4 ounces of lime water.
1 teaspoon of sugar.

Two teaspoons of lactose or corn sirup may be used to replace the sugar and one large can of evaporated cow's milk can be used with one can of water to replace the fresh milk. The foal should be fed about one-half pint every hour. Give large foals slightly more than a pint. After 4 or 5 days increase the interval to 2 hours. After a week, feed every 4 hours and increase the quantity accordingly.

FEEDING HORSES

Feeding practices vary from one locality to another—and among horsemen. The size of individual horses, the use to which they are put, the availability of feed, and the size of the enterprise also cause differences.

Fundamentally, the nature of horses remains the same. For this reason, successful feeding in one stable is not much different from successful feeding in another stable.

Skill and good judgment are essential in feeding horses. Horsemen may secure widely different results under similar conditions. Horses may be in the best of condition in one stable and have animation, nerve, speed, and endurance. In another stable, listless animals with dull eyes and rough coats testify to lack of judgment in their feeding and management. The unsatisfactory condition in the latter stable may not mean that the owner tried to economize on feed; horsemen who feed their animals the most economically may have the best horses.

The Digestive System

The alimentary canal includes the entire tube extending from the mouth to the rectum. Figure 55 and table 2 show the comparative

TABLE 2.—*Capacities of digestive tracts of horse, cow, and pig* [1]

Parts of digestive tract	Horse	Cow	Pig
	Quarts	*Quarts*	*Quarts*
Stomach	8 to 16		6 to 8
Rumen (paunch)		160	
Reticulum (honeycomb)		10	
Omasum (manyplies)		15	
Abomasum (true stomach of cow)		15	
Small intestine	48	62	9
Cecum	28 to 32		
Large intestine	80	40	10

[1] Values are for average size horses of 1,000 to 1,200 lb.

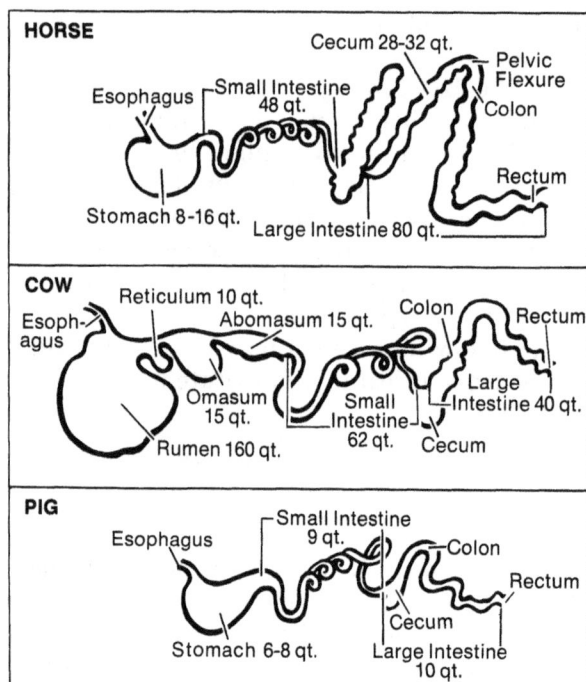

BN–37792

FIGURE 55.—Digestive tracts of the horse, cow, and pig.

structures and sizes of the digestive tracts of farm animals. As noted, the digestive tract of a horse is anatomically and physiologically quite different from that of a ruminant. The digestive tract of horses is much smaller, with the result that horses cannot eat as much roughage as cattle. Also, the primary seats of microbial activity in ruminants and horses occupy different locations in the digestive system in relation to the small intestine. In cows and sheep, the rumen precedes the small intestine; in horses, the cecum follows it.

Both the amount of bacterial synthesis and the efficiency of absorption of nutrients synthesized by the micro-organisms are likely to be lower in a horse than in a ruminant. In comparison to a cow, therefore, a horse should be fed less roughage, more and higher quality protein (no urea), and added B vitamins. Actually, the nutrient requirements of a horse appear more nearly parallel to those of a pig than a cow.

Recommended Nutrient Allowances

Unfortunately, little experimental work has been done on the minimum nutritional require-

ments of horses. However, presently available information indicates that the nutrient allowances recommended in tables 3 and 4 will meet the minimum requirements for horses and provide a reasonable margin of safety. A margin of safety is important owing to (1) variations in feed composition because of the soil on which it was grown, stage of maturity when it was harvested, amount of weathering, and losses in processing and storage; and (2) differences in environment and individual animals.

Minerals

The classical horse ration of grass, grass hay, and farm grains is usually deficient in calcium, but adequate in phosphorus. Also, salt is almost always deficient; and many horse rations do not contain sufficient iodine. Thus, horses usually need special mineral supplements. But do not feed them either more or less minerals than needed.

On the average, a horse will consume about 3 ounces of salt daily or 1⅓ pounds per week, although the salt requirements vary with work and temperature.

The salt requirements, and any calcium or phosphorus requirements not met by feeds, can

TABLE 3.—*Recommended allowances of protein, fiber, and total digestible nutrients (TDN)*

Type of horse	Minimum crude protein	Maximum crude fiber	Minimum TDN
	Percent	*Percent*	*Percent*
Most mature horses used for race, show, or pleasure	12	25	[1] 53 to 70
Broodmares	13	25	50 to 60
Stallions	14	25	[2] 50 to 68
Young equines:			
Foals, 2 weeks to 10 months old	21	8	68 to 74
Weanlings to 18 months old	14	20	60
18 months to 3 years old	13	25	50 to 60

[1] The heavier the work, the more energy is required.
[2] Increase the energy immediately before and during the breeding season.

TABLE 4.—*Recommended allowances of minerals and vitamins*

Kind of mineral or vitamin	Daily allowance per 1,000-pound horse [1]	Allowance per ton of finished feed (hay and grain combined) [2]
Minerals:		
Salt _____	2 oz.	10 lb.
Calcium _____	70.0 g.	12.33 lb.
Phosphorus _____	60.0 g.	10.57 lb.
Magnesium _____	3,200 mg.	256 g.
Iron _____	640 mg.	51.2 g.
Zinc _____	400 mg.	32.0 g.
Manganese _____	340 mg.	27.2 g.
Copper _____	90 mg.	7.2 g.
Iodine _____	2.6 mg.	.21 g.
Cobalt _____	1.5 mg.	.12 g.
Vitamins:		
Vitamin A _____USP__	50,000	4,000,000
Vitamin D_2 _____USP__	7,000	560,000
Vitamin E _____IU__	200	16,000
Choline _____mg__	400	32,000
Pantothenic acid__mg__	60	4,800
Niacin _____mg__	50	4,000
Riboflavin _____mg__	40	3,200
Thiamine (B_1) ___mg__	25	2,000
Vitamin K _____mg__	8	640
Folic acid _____mg__	2.5	200
Vitamin B_{12} _____μg [3]__	125	10,000

[1] This is based on an allowance of 25 pounds of feed per 1,000-pound horse per day, or 2.5 pounds of feed per 100 pounds of body weight.

[2] Where hay is fed separately, double this amount should be added to the concentrate.

[3] Micrograms.

best be supplied by allowing free access to a two-compartment box containing minerals. One compartment should have iodized salt and the other should contain a suitable mineral mixture.

It is important to have slightly more calcium than phosphorus in horse rations. Although the correct calcium to phosphorus ratio is not known, it is suggested that it be kept at between one to two parts calcium to one part phosphorus. A ration low in calcium and high in phosphorus may cause osteomalacia in mature horses. This condition may develop when rations with a Ca:P ratio of 0.8 to 1 are fed 6 to 12 months, and it will progress rapidly when the ratio is 0.6 to 1. Either a home-mixed or a commercial mineral may be used.

Vitamins

Certain vitamins are necessary to the growth, development, health, and reproduction of horses. Deficiencies of vitamins A and D are sometimes encountered. Also, indications are that vitamin E and some of the B vitamins (riboflavin and perhaps thiamine) are required by horses. Further, it is recognized that single, uncomplicated vitamin deficiencies are the exception rather than the rule.

High-quality, leafy, green forages plus plenty of sunshine generally give horses most of the vitamins they need. Horses get carotene (which the animal can convert to vitamin A) and riboflavin from green pasture and green hay not over a year old. Horses get vitamin D from sunlight and sun-cured hay.

Severe deficiency of vitamin A may cause night blindness, reproductive difficulties, poor or uneven hoof development, difficulty in breathing, incoordination, and poor appetite. There is also some evidence that deficiency of this vitamin may cause or contribute to certain leg bone weaknesses. When vitamin A deficiency symptoms appear, the horseman should add a stabilized vitamin A product to the ration.

Foals sometimes develop rickets because of insufficient vitamin D, calcium, or phosphorus. This can be prevented by exposing the animal to direct sunlight as much as possible, by allowing it free access to a suitable mineral mixture, or by providing it with good-quality sun-cured hay or luxuriant pasture grown on well-fertilized soil. In northern areas that do not have adequate sunshine, many horsemen provide the foal with a vitamin D supplement.

Horses seem to require vitamin E. Most practical rations contain liberal quantities of it, perhaps enough except under conditions of work stress or reproduction, or where there is interference with its utilization. Rather than buy and use costly vitamin E concentrates indiscriminately, add them to the ration only on the advice of a nutritionist or veterinarian.

A deficiency of riboflavin may cause periodic

ophthalmia (moon blindness), but it is known that lack of this vitamin is not the only factor in producing this condition. Sometimes moon blindness follows leptospirosis in horses and it may be caused by a localized hypersensitivity or allergic reaction. Periodic ophthalmia caused by lack of riboflavin may be prevented by feeding green hay and green pasture, supplying feeds high in riboflavin, or by adding crystalline riboflavin to the ration at the rate of 40 mg. per horse per day.

A thiamine deficiency has been observed in horses fed on poor quality hay and grain. Although sufficient thiamine may be synthesized in the digestive system, the amount absorbed may not always meet the full requirements. Other vitamins of the B complex may be essential. Healthy horses usually get enough of them either in natural rations or by synthesis in the intestinal tract. When neither green pasture nor high-quality dry roughage is available, B vitamins may be provided by adding to the ration distillers dried solubles, dried brewers yeast, or animal liver meal.

Water

Horses should have ample quantities of clean, fresh, cool water. They will drink 10 to 12 gallons daily; the amount depends on weather, amount of work done, and rations fed.

Free access to water is desirable. When this is not possible, horses should be watered at approximately the same times daily. Opinions vary among horsemen as to the proper times and method of watering horses. All agree, however, that regularity and frequency are desirable. Most horsemen agree that water may be given before, during, or after feeding.

Frequent, small waterings between feedings are desirable during warm weather or when the animal is being put to hard use. Do not allow a horse to drink heavily when he is hot, because he may founder; and do not allow a horse to drink heavily just before being put to work.

Home-Mixed Feeds

A horse feeding guide is given in table 5. In selecting rations, compare them with commercial feeds. If only small quantities are required

or little storage space is available, it may be more satisfactory to buy ready-mixed feeds.

When home-mixed feeds are used, feeds of similar nutritive properties can be interchanged in the ration as price relationships warrant. This makes it possible to obtain a balanced ration at lowest cost. Among the feeds that may be interchanged are grains such as oats, corn, barley, wheat, and sorghum; protein supplements such as linseed meal, soybean meal, and cottonseed meal; and hays of many varieties.

More than one kind of hay provides variety and appetite appeal. In season, any good pasture can replace part or all of the hay unless work or training conditions make substitution impractical.

During winter months, add a few sliced carrots to the suggested ration, an occasional bran mash, or a small amount of linseed meal. Also, use bran mash or linseed meal to regulate the bowels.

The proportion of concentrates must be increased and the roughages decreased as energy needs rise with a greater amount of work. A horse that works at a trot needs considerably more feed than one that works at a walk. For this reason, riding horses in medium to light use require somewhat less grain and more hay in proportion to body weight than horses that are racing.

In feeding horses, as with other classes of livestock, it is recognized that nutritional deficiencies (especially deficiencies of certain vitamins and minerals) may not be of sufficient proportions to cause clear-cut deficiency symptoms. Yet, such deficiencies without outward signs may cause great economic losses because they go unnoticed and unrectified. Accordingly, sufficient additives (especially minerals and vitamins) should always be present, but care should be taken to avoid imbalances.

Commercial Feeds

Commercial feeds are feeds mixed by manufacturers who specialize in the feed business. Today, about 60 million tons of commercial feeds are marketed each year.

Commercial feed manufacturers are able to

purchase feed in quantity lots, making possible price advantages and the scientific control of quality. Many horsemen have found that because of the small quantities of feed usually involved, and the complexities of horse rations, they have more reason to rely on good commercial feeds than do owners of other classes of farm animals.

Currently, horsemen are much interested in complete, all-pelleted feed, in which the hay and grain are combined. Pelleted feeds may be prepared from concentrates alone, forage alone, or concentrates and roughage combined in a complete ration.

Compared to conventional long hay and grain concentrate fed separately, all-pelleted feed has the following advantages:

(1) It is less bulky and easier to store and handle, thus lessening transportation, building, and labor costs. Pelleted roughage requires one-fifth to one-third as much space as is required by the same roughage in loose or chopped form.

(2) Pelleting prevents horses from selectively refusing ingredients likely to be high in certain dietary essentials; each bite is a balanced feed.

(3) Pelleting practically eliminates waste; therefore, less pelleted feed is required. Horses may waste up to 20 percent of long hay. Waste of conventional feed is highest where low quality hay is fed or feed containers are poorly designed.

(4) Pelleting eliminates dustiness and lessens the likelihood of heaves.

(5) Pellet-fed horses are trimmer in the middle and more attractive because they consume less bulk.

The following points are pertinent to the proper understanding and use of all-pelleted rations:

(1) One-half-inch pellets are preferred for mature horses, and one-fourth-inch pellets for weanlings and short yearlings. Also, very hard pellets should be avoided; if horses cannot chew them, they will not eat them.

(2) The ratio of roughage to concentrates should be higher in all-pelleted rations than when long hay is fed. For most horses, the ratio may range from 60.5 percent roughage to 39.5

percent concentrate up to 69 percent roughage to 31 percent concentrate.

(3) Any horse feed should form a loose mass in the stomach to assure ease of digestion, fewer digestive disturbances, and less impaction. To this end, in a complete all-pelleted ration, such feeds as oats and barley should be crimped or steam rolled but not finely ground. The roughage should be 1/4-inch chop or coarser. Otherwise, a couple of pounds of long hay may be fed daily to each horse.

(4) Young horses and horses at heavy work need more energy. They should be fed less roughage and more concentrate.

(5) When less roughage and more concentrate is fed, horses are likely to be overfed and get too fat if they are idle or at light to medium work. But if the total feed consumption is limited too severely to keep the weight down, the problem of wood chewing is increased because of a lack of physical filling of the digestive tract.

(6) When the roughage consists of high quality legume hay, a higher percentage of roughage may be used than when all or part of the roughage is grass or other nonlegumes.

(7) If more energy is needed for racing or young stock on an all-pelleted ration, it can be provided either by increasing the daily allowance of the all-pelleted ration, and/or replacing a portion of the all-pelleted ration with a suitable concentrate or supplement.

(8) Because waste is eliminated, less all-pelleted feed is required than conventional feed. For a horse at light work, give 14 to 18 pounds of all-pelleted feed daily per 1,000 pounds of body weight. Use a feed that contains 51 to 58 percent total digestible nutrients (TDN). Increase the feed allowance with the severity of work.

(9) As with any change in feed, the switch to an all-pelleted ration should be made gradually, otherwise such vices as wood chewing and bolting (eating feed too rapidly) may be induced. At first, continue to offer all the long hay the horse wants and slowly replace the grain portion of the conventional ration with the complete pelleted feed. Increase the pelleted feed by 1 to 2 pounds daily and begin gradually lessening the hay. After a few days, the horse

TABLE 5.—*Light horse feeding guide*

Age, sex, and use	Daily allowance	Kind of hay	Suggested grain rations		
			Rations No. 1	Rations No. 2	Rations No. 3
			Pounds	*Pounds*	*Pounds*
Stallions in breeding season (weighing 900 to 1,400 lb.).	¾ to 1½ lb. grain per 100 lb. body weight, together with a quantity of hay within same range.	Grass-legume mixed; or ⅓ to ½ legume hay, with remainder grass hay.	Oats _____ 55 Wheat _____ 20 Wheat bran __ 20 Linseed meal _ 5	Corn _____ 35 Oats _____ 35 Wheat _____ 15 Wheat bran __ 15	Oats _____100
Pregnant mares (weighing 900 to 1,400 lb.).	¾ to 1½ lb. grain per 100 lb. body weight, together with a quantity of hay within same range.	Grass-legume mixed; or ⅓ to ½ legume hay, with remainder grass hay (straight grass hay may be used first half of pregnancy).	Oats _____ 80 Wheat bran __ 20	Barley _____ 45 Oats _____ 45 Wheat bran __ 10	Oats _____ 95 Linseed meal _ 5
Foals before weaning (weighing 100 to 350 lb. with projected mature weights of 900 to 1,400 lb.).	½ to ¾ lb. grain per 100 lb. body weight, together with a quantity of hay within same range.	Legume hay ____	Oats _____ 50 Wheat bran __ 40 Linseed meal _ 10	Oats _____ 30 Barley _____ 30 Wheat bran __ 30 Linseed meal _ 10	Oats _____ 80 Wheat bran __ 20
			Rations balanced on basis of following assumption: Mares of mature weights of 600, 800, 1,000, and 1,200 lb. may produce 36, 42, 44, and 49 lb. of milk daily.		
Weanlings (weighing 350 to 450 lb.).	1 to 1½ lb. grain and 1½ to 2 lb. hay per 100 lb. body weight.	Grass-legume mixed; or ½ legume hay, with remainder grass hay.	Oats _____ 30 Barley _____ 30 Wheat bran __ 30 Linseed meal _ 10	Oats _____ 70 Wheat bran __ 15 Linseed meal _ 15	Oats _____ 80 Linseed meal _ 20
Yearlings, 2d summer (weighing 450 to 700 lb.).	Good, luxuriant pasture (if in training or for other reasons without access to pasture, the ration should be intermediate between the adjacent upper and lower groups).				
Yearlings, or rising 2-year-olds, second winter (weighing 700 to 1,000 lb.).	½ to 1 lb. grain and 1 to 1½ lb. hay per 100 lb. body weight.	Grass-legume mixed; or ⅓ to ½ legume hay, with remainder grass hay.	Oats _____ 80 Wheat bran __ 20	Barley _____ 35 Oats _____ 35 Bran _____ 15 Linseed meal _ 15	Oats _____100

See note at end of table.

usually will stop eating the hay and it can be removed completely from the ration.

(10) The feces of pellet-fed horses are softer than the feces of those not fed pellets.

Among many horsemen, the feeling persists that horses fed all-pelleted rations are more

TABLE 5.—*Light horse feeding guide*—Continued

Age, sex, and use	Daily allowance	Kind of hay	Suggested grain rations		
			Rations No. 1	Rations No. 2	Rations No. 3
			Pounds	*Pounds*	*Pounds*
Light horses at work; riding, driving, and racing (weighing 900 to 1,400 lb.).	Hard use—1¼ to 1⅓ lb. grain and 1 to 1¼ lb. hay per 100 lb. body weight. Medium use — ¾ to 1 lb. grain and 1 to 1¼ lb. hay per 100 lb. body weight. Light use—⅖ to ½ lb. grain and 1¼ to 1½ lb. hay per 100 lb. body weight.	Grass hay _____	Oats _____100	Oats _____ 70 Corn _____ 30	Oats _____ 70 Barley _____ 30
Mature idle horses; stallions, mares, and geldings (weighing 900 to 1,400 lb.).	1½ to 1¾ lb. hay per 100 lb. body weight.	Pasture in season; or grass-legume mixed hay.	(With grass hay, add ¾ lb. of a high protein supplement daily.)		

Note.—With all rations and for all classes and ages of horses, provide free access to separate containers of (1) iodized salt and (2) a mixture of 1 part salt and 2 parts steamed bonemeal or other suitable calcium-phosphorous supplement.

likely to chew wood than those fed long hay. This may be true to some degree. But some horses will chew wood regardless of what they are fed. This leads to the conclusion that the way to prevent wood chewing is simply to use metal, masonry, or other nonwood materials for all buildings, fences, and other equipment. Of course, this is not always practical.

Wood chewing can be lessened, although not prevented entirely, through one or more of the following practices:

(1) Increase the exercise.

(2) Feed three times a day, rather than twice a day, even though the total daily feed allowance remains the same.

(3) Spread out the pellets in a larger feed container or place a few large stones about the size of a baseball in the feed container, thereby making the horse work harder and longer to obtain the pellets.

(4) Provide 2 to 4 pounds of straw or coarse grass hay per animal per day, thereby giving the horse something to nibble on when he is idle.

How to Feed

Feeding horses is both an art and a science. The art is knowing how to feed and how to take care of each horse's individual requirements. The science is meeting the nutritive requirements with the right combination of ingredients.

Amount to feed

Because the horse has a limited digestive capacity, the amount of concentrates must be increased and the roughages decreased when the energy needs rise with more work. The following general guides may be used for the daily ration of horses under usual conditions.

Horses at light work (1 to 3 hours per day of riding or driving).—Allow two-fifths to one-half pound of grain and 1¼ to 1½ pounds of hay per day per 100 pounds of body weight.

Horses at medium work (3 to 5 hours per day of riding or driving).—Allow about three-fourths of a pound of grain and 1 to 1¼ pounds of hay per 100 pounds of body weight.

Horses at hard work (5 to 8 hours per day of riding or driving).—Allow about 1¼ to 1⅓ pounds of grain and 1 to 1¼ pounds of hay per 100 pounds of body weight.

As will be noted from these recommendations, the total allowance of both concentrates and hay should be about 2 to 2½ pounds daily per 100 pounds of body weight.

About 6 to 12 pounds of grain daily is an average grain ration for a light horse at medium or light work. Racehorses in training usually consume 10 to 16 pounds of grain per day; the exact amount varies with the individual requirements and the amount of work. The hay allowance averages about 1 to 1¼ pounds daily per 100 pounds of body weight, but it is restricted as the grain allowance is increased. Light feeders should not be overworked.

The quantities of feeds recommended are intended as guides only. The allowance, especially the concentrates, should be increased when the horse is too thin and decreased when the horse is too fat.

Starting horses on feed

Horses must be accustomed to changes in feed gradually. In general, they may be given as much nonlegume roughage as they will consume. But they must be accustomed gradually to high-quality legumes, which may be very laxative. This can be done by slowly replacing the nonlegume roughage with greater quantities of legumes. Also, as the grain ration is increased, the roughage is decreased.

Starting horses on grain requires care and good judgment. Usually it is advisable first to accustom them to a bulky type of ration; a starting ration with considerable rolled oats is excellent for this purpose.

The keenness of the appetite and the consistency of the droppings are an excellent index of a horse's capacity to take more feed. In all instances, scouring should be avoided.

Frequency, regularity, and order of feeding

The grain ration usually is divided into three equal feeds given morning, noon, and night. Because a digestive tract distended with hay is a hindrance in hard work, most of the hay should be fed at night. The common practice is to feed one-fourth of the daily hay allowance at each of the morning and noon feedings and the remaining one-half at night when the animals have plenty of time to eat leisurely.

Horses learn to anticipate their feed. Accordingly, they should be fed at the same time each day. During warm weather, they will eat better if the feeding hours are early and late, in the cool of the day.

Usually the grain ration is fed first and then the roughage. This way, the animals can eat the bulky roughages more leisurely.

Sudden changes in diet should be avoided, especially when changing from a less concentrated ration to a more concentrated one. If this rule of feeding is ignored, horses have digestive disturbances and go "off feed." When ingredients are added or omitted, the change should be made gradually. Likewise, caution should be exercised in turning horses to pasture or in transferring them to more lush grazing.

Attention to details

A successful horseman pays great attention to details. In addition to maintaining the health and comfort of his animals, he also considers their individual likes and temperaments. Nervousness and inefficient use of feed are caused by excessive exercise to the point of undue fatigue and stress, rough treatment, noise, and excitement.

General feeding rules

Observance of the following rules will help avoid some of the common difficulties that result from poor feeding practices:

(1) Know the approximate weight and age of each animal.

(2) Never feed moldy, musty, dusty, or frozen feed.

(3) Inspect the feed box frequently to see if the horse goes off feed.

(4) Keep the feed and water containers clean.

(5) Make certain that the horse's teeth are sound.

(6) Do not feed concentrates to a hot horse; allow time for his feed to digest before he is worked.

(7) Feed horses as individuals. Learn the peculiarities and desires of each animal because each one is different.

(8) See that horses get enough exercise. It improves their appetite, digestion, and overall well-being.

(9) Do not feed from the hand; this can lead to "nibbling."

Horses fitted for show or sale should be let down in condition gradually. Many horsemen accomplish this difficult task, and yet retain strong vigorous animals, by cutting down gradually on the feed and increasing the exercise.

Signs of a well-fed, healthy horse

The signs of a well-fed, healthy horse are listed as follows:

Contentment.—The horse looks completely unworried when resting.

Alertness.—The horse is "bright eyed and bushy tailed," and he will perk up his ears at the slightest provocation.

Good appetite.—The appetite is good, as indicated by neighing and pawing before he is fed and attacking the feed with relish.

Sleek coat and pliable, elastic skin.—A sleek coat and a pliable, elastic skin characterize a healthy horse. When the hair loses its luster and the skin becomes dry, scurfy, and hidebound, usually trouble is ahead.

Pink eye membranes.—The eye membranes, which can be seen when the lower lid is pulled down, should be pink and moist.

Normal feces and urine.—The consistency of the feces varies with the diet. For example, lush pasture usually causes looseness, and pellets generally cause moist feces. Neither extreme dryness nor scouring should exist. Both the feces and urine should be passed without effort and free of blood, mucus, or pus.

Normal temperature, pulse, and breathing.— The average rectal temperature of horses is 100.5° F., with a range of 99° to 100.8°. The normal pulse rate is 32 to 44 beats per minute, and the normal breathing rate is 8 to 16 breaths per minute.

In general, any marked and persistent deviations from these normals are signs of ill health.

Pastures

It is becoming difficult to provide good pasture for horses, especially in suburban areas. The use of a temporary pasture grown in regular crop rotation is recommended instead of a permanent pasture that may become infested with parasites. Legume pasture is excellent for horses because they are less subject to bloat than cattle or sheep. The specific grass or grass-legume mixture will vary from area to area according to differences in soil, temperature, and rainfall. Your county agricultural agent or a specialist at your State agricultural college can furnish recommendations for pastures.

Horse pastures should be well drained and not too rough or stony. All dangerous places such as pits, stumps, poles, and tanks should be guarded. Shade, water, and suitable minerals should be available in all pastures.

Most horse pastures can be improved by seeding new and better varieties of grasses and legumes and by fertilizing and management. Also, horsemen need to give attention to supplementing some pastures with additional feed. Pastures early in the season have a high water content and lack energy. Mature, weathered grass is almost always deficient in protein, with as little as 3 percent or less, and low in carotene, the precursor of vitamin A. However, these deficiencies can be corrected by proper supplemental feeding.

Feeding the Broodmare

Regular and normal reproduction is the basis for profit on any horse breeding establishment. However, only 40 to 60 percent of mares bred produce foals. There are many causes of reproductive failure, but inadequate nutrition is a major one. The following pointers are pertinent to feeding a broodmare properly:

(1) Condition the mare for breeding by providing adequate and proper feed and the right

amount of exercise prior to the breeding season.

(2) See that adequate proteins, minerals, and vitamins are available during the last third of pregnancy when the fetus grows most rapidly.

(3) Lessen and lighten the ration at and after foaling; give less feed and add some wheat bran to the feed. During cool weather, it is important to take the chill off water at foaling time.

(4) Provide adequate nutrition during lactation, because the requirements during this period are more rigorous than the requirements during pregnancy.

(5) Make sure that young growing mares receive adequate nutrients; otherwise, the fetus

will not develop properly or the dam will not produce milk except at the expense of her body tissues.

Feeding the Stallion

The ration exerts a powerful effect on sperm production and semen quality. Successful breeders adhere to the following rules:

(1) Feed a balanced ration, giving particular attention to proteins, minerals, and vitamins.

(2) Regulate the feed allowance because the stallion can become infertile if he gets too fat. Also, increase the exercise when the stallion is not a sure breeder.

(3) Provide pasture in season as a source of both nutrients and exercise.

MANAGEMENT OF HORSES

Horse management practices vary between areas and individual horsemen. In general, however, the principles of good management are the same everywhere.

Stable Management

The following stable management practices are recommended:

(1) Remove the top layer of clay floors yearly; replace with fresh clay, then level and tamp. Keep the stable floor higher than the surrounding area so the floor will stay dry.

(2) Keep stalls well lighted.

(3) Use properly constructed hay racks to lessen waste and contamination of hay. Do not have hay racks in maternity stalls.

(4) Scrub concentrate containers as often as necessary and always after feeding a wet mash.

(5) Remove excrement and wet or soiled material from the bedding daily, and provide fresh bedding.

(6) Practice strict stable sanitation to prevent fecal contamination of feed and water.

(7) Lead foals when taking them from the stall to the paddock and back as a way to further their training.

(8) Restrict the ration when horses are idle, and provide either a wet bran mash the evening before an idle day or turn idle horses to pasture.

(9) Provide proper ventilation at all times by means of open doors, windows that open in-

wardly from the top, or stall partitions slatted at the top.

(10) Keep stables in repair at all times to lessen injury hazards.

Kind and amount of bedding

Select bedding material by availability and price, absorptive capacity, and potential value as a fertilizer. Bedding should not be dusty, too coarse, or too easily kicked aside. Cereal grain straw or wood shavings generally make the best bedding material.

A soft, comfortable bed should insure proper rest. The animal will be much easier to groom if his bedding is kept clean. A minimum daily allowance of clean bedding is 10 to 15 pounds per animal.

Ways of handling horse manure

Clay floors cannot be cleaned by flushing with water, and hard stable floors of concrete, asphalt, or wood require considerable bedding to provide softness and comfort. These conditions make it impractical to handle horse manure as a liquid. But horse manure is relatively dry and well adapted to handling as a solid.

In large horse establishments, the use of automatic gutter cleaners can eliminate much of the hand labor in handling manure as a solid. Automatic gutter cleaners may be (1) located in the alleyway or immediately outside the barn, (2) covered except for trapdoors, and

(3) designed to carry the manure from the gutter directly into a spreader.

Some large establishments fork the manure from the stalls into the alley and then load it by means of a scraper or power loader. But this method is more messy and less convenient than an automatic gutter cleaner.

Both small and large horse establishments face the problem of what to do with horse manure after it is removed from the stable. Because the feces of horses are the primary source of infection by internal parasites, fresh horse manure should never be spread on pastures grazed by horses. The alternatives for the disposal of horse manure are as follows:

(1) Spread fresh manure on fields that will be plowed and cropped if there is sufficient land and this is feasible.

(2) Contract with a nearby vegetable grower to remove the manure.

(3) Store the manure in a tightly constructed pit for at least 2 weeks before spreading it; this allows the spontaneously generated heat to destroy the parasites.

(4) Compost the manure in an area where it will neither pollute a stream nor offend the neighbors; then spread it on the land.

Care of the Feet

The value of a horse lies chiefly in his ability to move; therefore, good feet and legs are necessary. The important points in the care of a horse's feet are to keep them clean, prevent them from drying out, trim them so they retain proper shape and length, and shoe them correctly when shoes are needed.

Each day, clean the feet of horses that are shod, stabled, or worked and inspect them for loose shoes and thrush. Thrush is a disease of the foot caused by a fungus and characterized by a pungent odor. It causes a deterioration of tissues in the cleft of the frog or in the junction between the frog and bars. This disease produces lameness and can be serious if not treated.

Trimming and shoeing

Before trimming or shoeing, a horseman should be able to recognize proper and faulty conformation. Figure 56 shows the proper posture of the hoof and incorrect postures caused by hoofs grown too long either in toe or heel. The slope is considered normal when the toe of the hoof and the pastern have the same direction. This angle should be kept in mind and changed only as a corrective measure. If it should become necessary to correct uneven wear of the hoof, correct gradually over a period of several trimmings.

Before the feet are trimmed, the horse should be inspected while standing squarely on a level, hard surface. Then he should be seen at both the walk and the trot.

The hoofs should be trimmed every month or 6 weeks whether the animal is shod or not. If shoes are left on too long, the hoofs grow out of proportion. This may throw the horse off balance and put extra stress on the tendons. Always keep the hoofs at proper length and

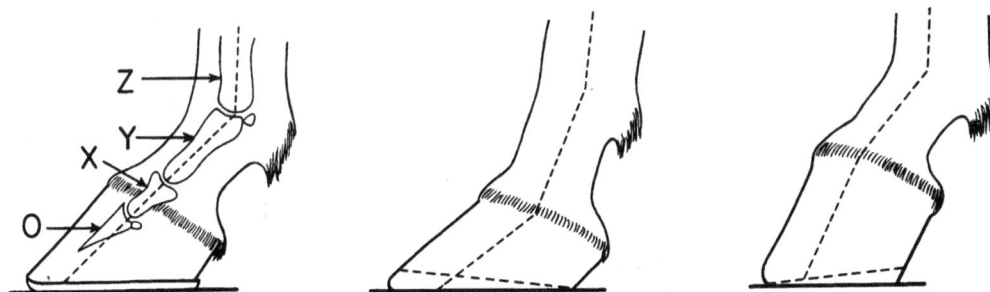

BN-5966

FIGURE 56.—Left, properly trimmed hoof with normal foot axis: O, Coffin bone; X, short pastern bone; Y, long pastern bone; Z, cannon bone. Center, toe too long, which breaks the foot axis backward; horizontal dotted line shows how hoof should be trimmed to restore normal posture. Right, heel too long, which breaks the foot axis forward; horizontal dotted line shows how trimming will restore the correct posture.

correct posture. Trim the hoofs near the level of the sole; otherwise, they will split off if the horse remains unshod. Trim the frog carefully and remove only ragged edges that allow filth to accumulate in the crevices. Trim the sole very sparingly, if at all, and never rasp the wall of the hoof.

The following list describes the common faults of the foot and tells how to correct them by proper trimming.

Splayfoot.—The front toes are turned out and the heels are turned in. Trim the outer half of the foot.

Pigeon-toe.—The front toes are turned in and the heels are turned out, the opposite of splayfoot. Trim the inner half of the foot more heavily; leave the outer half relatively long.

Quarter crack.—A vertical crack appears on the side of the hoof. Keep the hoof moist. Shorten the toe of the hoof and use a corrective shoe.

Cocked ankles.—The horse stands with the fetlocks bent forward, most frequently the hind ones. Lower the heels to correct. However, raising the heels gives the horse more immediate comfort.

Contracted heels.—The heels are contracted or shrunken. Lower the heels and allow the frog to carry more of the weight. This tends to spread the heels apart.

Horses should be shod when they are used on hard surfaces for any length of time. Also, shoes may be used to change gaits and action, correct faulty hoof structure or growth, protect the hoof from such conditions as corns, contraction, or cracks, and aid in gripping the track. Shoes should be made to fit the foot and not the foot to fit the shoe. Reshoe or reset at 4- to 6-week intervals. Do not attempt to shoe a horse without first getting instructions from a farrier.

Care of the foal's feet

Foals may damage their limbs when the weight is not equally distributed because of unshapely hoofs. On the other hand, faulty limbs may be helped or even corrected if the hoofs are trimmed regularly. Also, trimming helps educate the foal and makes shoeing easier at maturity. If the foal is run on pasture, trim-ming the feet may be necessary long before weaning time. A good practice is to check the feet every month or 6 weeks and, if necessary, trim a small amount each time rather than a large amount at one time. Tendons should not become strained because of incorrectly trimmed feet. Usually, only the bottom rim of the hoof should be trimmed, although sometimes the heel, frog, or toe of the hoof may need trimming. The hoofs are trimmed with a rasp, farrier's knife, and nippers. A rasp is used more than the other tools.

Before the feet are trimmed, the foal should first be inspected while standing squarely on a hard surface and then inspected at the walk and the trot.

Treatment of dry hoofs

Hoofs may become dry and brittle; sometimes they split and cause lameness. The frogs lose their elasticity and are no longer effective shock absorbers. If the dryness is prolonged, the frogs shrink and the heels contract.

Dry hoofs usually can be prevented by packing them with a specially prepared formulation, applying a good hoof dressing, keeping the ground wet around the watering tank, and/or attaching wet burlap sacks around them.

Exercise

Horses should exercise as much as possible on pasture. They will develop strong, sound feet and legs from outdoor exercise. If no pasture is available, exercise mature animals for an hour or two a day under saddle or in harness.

Horses with bad feet frequently cannot exercise on roads. Those with faulty tendons may not be able to exercise under saddle. Allow these animals to exercise in a large paddock, by longeing on a 30- to 40-foot rope, or by leading.

Transporting Horses

Horses can be transported by trailer, van, truck, rail, boat, or plane. Most horses are transported in a one- or two-horse trailer drawn behind a car or truck. The requisites for good motor transportation, regardless of type, are as follows:

Provide good footing.—The floor of the vehicle should be covered with heavy coco matting made for the purpose, sand covered with straw or other suitable bedding material, or rubber mats. Clean the floor covering at frequent intervals while in transit to avoid ammonia and heat.

Drive carefully.—Drive at a moderate, constant speed as distinguished from fast or jerky driving, which causes added stress and tiring. If weather conditions make the roads unsafe, the vehicle should be stopped.

Make nurse stops.—Nurse stops should be made at about 3-hour intervals when mares and foals are transported together.

Provide proper ventilation.—Provide plenty of fresh air without drafts.

Teach horses to load early in life.—When horses will be transported later in life, they should be accustomed to transportation as youngsters before they get too big and strong. This can be done by moving them from one part of the farm to another.

Provide health certificate and statement of ownership.—A health certificate signed by a licensed veterinarian is required for most interstate shipments. Foreign shipments must be accompanied by a health certificate that has been approved by a government veterinarian. This takes several days. Branded horses must be accompanied by a brand certificate, and all horses should be accompanied by a statement of ownership.

Schedule properly.—Schedule the transportation so that animals will arrive on time. Show, sale, and race animals should arrive a few days early.

Have the horses relaxed.—Horses ship best if they are relaxed and not overtired before they are moved.

Clean and disinfect public conveyance.—Before using any type of public conveyance, thoroughly clean and disinfect it. Steam is excellent for this purpose. Remove nails or other hazards that might cause injury.

Have a competent caretaker accompany horses.—Valuable horses should not be shipped in the care of an inexperienced person.

Use shanks except on stallions.—When animals are tied, use a ⅝-inch cotton rope shank that is 5 feet long and has a big swivel snap at the end. Chain shanks are too noisy. Always tie the shank with a knot that can easily and quickly be released in case of an emergency.

Feed lightly.—Allow horses only a half feed of grain before they are loaded for shipment and at the first feed after they reach their destination. In transit, horses should be given all the good quality hay they will eat, preferably alfalfa, to keep the bowels open, but no concentrates should be fed. Commercial hay nets or homemade burlap containers may be used to hold the hay in transit, but they should not be placed too high.

Water liberally.—When transporting horses, give them all the fresh, clean water they will drink at frequent intervals unless the weather is extremely hot and there is danger of gorging. A tiny bit of molasses may be added to each pail of water, beginning about a week before the horses are shipped, and the addition of molasses to the water may be continued in transit. This prevents any taste change in the water.

Pad the stalls.—Many experienced shippers favor padding the inside of the vehicle to lessen the likelihood of injury, especially when a valuable animal is shipped. Coco matting or a sack of straw properly placed may save the horse's hocks from injury.

Take along tools and supplies.—The following tools and supplies should be taken along in a suitable box: pinch bar, hammer, hatchet, saw, nails, pliers, flashlight, extra halters and shanks, twitch, canvas slapper or short piece of hose, pair of gloves, fork and broom, fire extinguisher, and medicine for colic and shipping fever provided by a veterinarian.

Check shoes, blankets, and bandages.—Whenever possible, ship horses barefoot. Never allow them to wear calked shoes during a long shipment. They may wear smooth shoes. In cool weather, horses may be blanketed if an attendant is present in case a horse gets entangled. The legs of racehorses in training should be bandaged to keep the ankles from getting scuffed or the tendons bruised. Bandages are not necessary on breeding stock except for valuable stallions and young animals. When bandages are used, they should be reset often.

Be calm when loading and unloading.—In loading and unloading horses, always be patient and never show anger. Try kindness first; pat the horse and speak to him to reassure him. If this fails, it may be necessary to use one of the following techniques:

(1) Sometimes the use of the twitch at the right time is desirable, especially if the horse is tossing his head about.

(2) When a horse must be disciplined, a canvas slapper or a short rubber hose can be used effectively; these make noise without causing much hurt.

(3) If a horse gets very excited and is about to break out, dash a bucket of water in his face; usually he will back off and calm down.

(4) A nervous, excitable horse may be calmed by a tranquilizer, which should be administered by a veterinarian.

(5) If a horse will not move or is kicking, grab his tail and push it over his back. In this position, he cannot kick but can be pushed along.

Control insects.—In season, flies and other insects molest animals in transit. When necessary, use a reliable insecticide to control insects. Follow directions on the container label.

BUILDINGS AND EQUIPMENT

Properly designed, constructed, and arranged horse buildings and equipment give increased animal comfort and performance, greater efficiency in the use of feed, and less expenditure of labor in the care of horses. Also, attractive barns add to the beauty of the landscape. In serving these purposes, barns need not be elaborate or expensive.

Buildings

The primary reasons for having horse buildings are (1) to provide a place in which to confine horses and store feed and tack and (2) to modify the environment by controlling temperature, humidity, and other factors.

Types and sizes of horse barns

Needs for housing horses and storage of materials vary according to the intended use of the buildings. Broadly speaking, horse barns are designed to serve either (1) small horse establishments that have one to a few animals, (2) large horse breeding establishments, or (3) riding, training, and boarding stables.

Various types and sizes of stalls and sheds are used in horse barns. However, in all types except the breeding shed, ceilings should be 9 feet high and doors should be 8 feet high and 4 feet wide. The breeding shed should have a ceiling 15 to 20 feet high and a door wide enough to permit entrance of vehicles.

The recommended plans for different kinds of horse barns are as follows:

Small horse establishments.—These horse barns are for housing pleasure horses or ponies or raising a few foals (fig. 57). Box stalls should be 12 feet square and tie stalls should be 5 feet wide and 10 or 12 feet long.

Build the stalls in a row and provide a combination tack and feed room for units with one or two stalls. Use separate tack and feed rooms for units with three or more stalls. Generally, not more than a 1-month supply of feed is stored at a time. The use of all-pelleted feed lessens storage space requirements.

Large horse-breeding establishments.—Large establishments need specially designed buildings for different purposes. They are as follows:

(1) *Broodmare and foaling barn.*—This can be a rectangular building either (a) with a central aisle and a row of stalls along each side or (b) of the "island" type with two rows of stalls back to back surrounded by an alley or runway. Most broodmare stalls are 12 feet square, although they may be up to 16 feet square. A stall 16 feet square is desirable for foaling. A broodmare barn needs an office for records; toilet facilities; hot water supply; veterinary supply room; tack room; and storage space for hay, bedding, and grain.

(2) *Stallion barn.*—This barn provides quarters for one or more stallions. It should have a small tack and equipment room, and it may or may not have feed storage. The stalls should be 14 feet square.

Provide a paddock near the barn or, if possible, adjacent to it. The paddock can be any shape but each side should be at least 300 feet long.

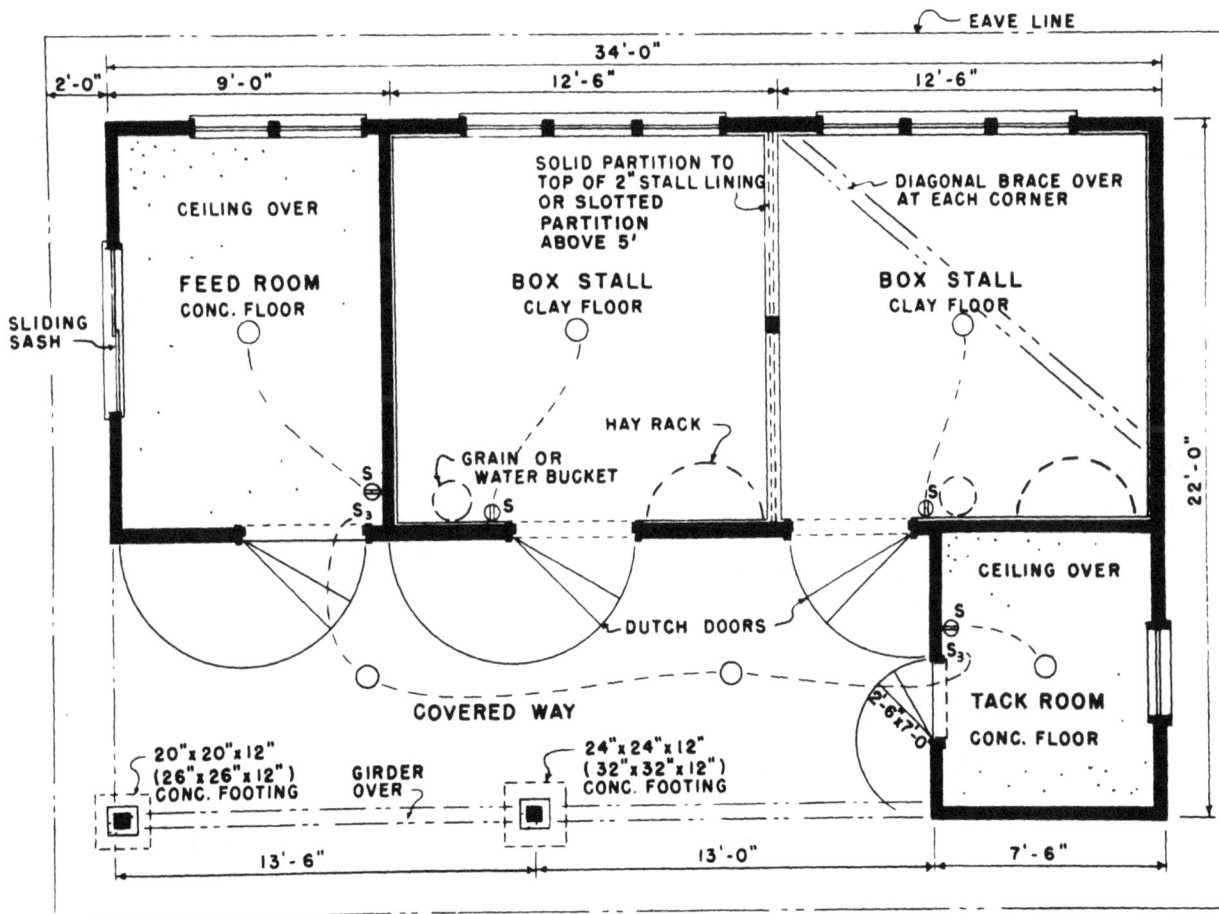

BN–5964; BN–5965

FIGURE 57.—Horse barn above and floor plan below. Barn has two box stalls, a feed room, and tack room.

(3) **Barren mare barn.**—Use an open shed or rectangular building that has a combination rack and trough down the center or along the wall. Provide storage space for hay, grain, and bedding. Allow each animal 150 square feet of space.

(4) **Weanling and yearling quarters.**—Either an open shed or a barn with stalls may be used. Both weanlings and yearlings may be kept in the same building, but different age and sex groups should be kept apart. When stalls are used, two weanlings or two yearlings may be kept together. Stalls should be 10 feet square.

(5) **Breeding shed.**—This should be a large, roofed enclosure that has a laboratory for the veterinarian, hot water facilities, and stalls for preparing mares for breeding and for holding foals. The shed should be 24 feet square.

(6) **Isolation quarters.**—These quarters are for sick animals and animals new to the farm. Use a small barn that has feed and water facilities and an adjacent paddock. Stalls should be 12 feet square.

Riding, training, and boarding stables.—For this purpose, the quarters may consist of (1) stalls constructed back to back in the center of the barn with an indoor ring around the stalls, (2) stalls built around the sides of the barn with the ring in the center, or (3) stalls on either side of a hallway or alleyway and the ring outdoors. Box stalls should be 10 to 12 feet square and tie stalls should be 5 feet wide and 10 to 12 feet long.

Environmental control

Animals perform better and require less feed if they are raised under ideal conditions of temperature, humidity, and ventilation. Environmental control is of particular importance in horse barn construction because many horses spend most of the time in a stall. The investment in environmental control facilities must be balanced against the expected increased returns because there is a point where further expenditures for environmental control will not increase returns sufficiently to justify added cost.

Before the building is designed, it is necessary to know how much heat and moisture a horse produces. Body heat production varies according to body weight, rate of feeding, environmental conditions, and degree of activity. Under average conditions, a 1,000-pound horse produces about 1,790 British thermal units (B.t.u.) per hour, and a 1,500-pound horse about 2,450 B.t.u. per hour. A horse breathes into the air approximately 17.5 pounds, or 2.1 gallons, of moisture per day.

Until more experimental information is available, the following environmental control recommendations, based on confinement systems used for other classes of animals, may be followed.

Temperature.—A range of 45° to 75° F. is satisfactory, with 55° considered best. Until a newborn foal is dry, it should be warmed to 75° to 80°. This can be done with a heat lamp.

Humidity.—A range of 50 to 75 percent relative humidity is acceptable with 60 percent preferred.

Ventilation.—The barn should have as little moisture and odor as possible, and it should be free from drafts. In a properly ventilated barn, the ventilation system should provide 60 cubic feet per minute (c.f.m.) for each 1,000 pounds of horse in winter and 160 c.f.m. per 1,000 pounds of horse in summer. In summer, satisfactory ventilation usually can be achieved by opening barn doors and by installing hinged walls or panels near the ceiling that swing open.

Requisites of horse barns

Whether a new horse layout is built or an old one is altered, all buildings, fences, corrals, and trees should be placed according to a master plan, for once established, they usually are difficult and expensive to move. The arrangement should make the best possible use of land and should require little walking by attendants when caring for horses.

All horse barns should meet the following requisites:

Accessibility.—Barns should be on an all-weather roadway or lane to facilitate the use of horses, delivery of feed and bedding, and removal of manure.

Dryness.—Barns should be on high ground so water will drain away from them.

Expandable design.—Barns should be

designed so they are easy to expand if and when the time comes. Often a building can be lengthened provided no other structures or utilities interfere.

Water and electricity.—Water and electricity should be available and convenient to use.

Controlled environment.—Barns should be built to modify winter and summer temperatures, maintain acceptable humidity and ventilation, minimize stress on the horses' nerves, and protect horses from rain, snow, sun, and wind.

Reasonable cost.—Initial cost is important but durability and maintenance should be considered, as well as such intangible values as pride and satisfaction in the buildings and advertising value.

Adequate space.—Too little space may jeopardize the health and well-being of horses, but too much space means unnecessary expense.

Storage areas.—Storage space for feed, bedding, and tack should be provided in the building where they are used.

Attractiveness.—An attractive horse barn increases the sale value of the property. A horse barn will have aesthetic value if it has good proportions and is in harmony with the natural surroundings.

Minimum fire risk.—The use of fire resistant materials gives added protection to horses. Also, fire retarding paints and sprays may be used.

Safety.—Projections that might injure horses should be removed. Feeding and watering equipment should be arranged so attendants need not walk behind horses.

Labor saving construction.—This requisite is a must in any commercial horse establishment. Also, where horses are kept for pleasure, unnecessary labor should be eliminated in feeding, cleaning, and handling.

Healthful living conditions.—Healthy horses are better performers; therefore, barns should be easy to keep clean so they will provide healthful living conditions.

Rodent and bird control.—Feed and tack storage areas should be rodent and bird proof.

Suitable corrals and paddocks.—Horse barns should have well-drained, safe, fenced corrals or paddocks adjacent to them. If this is not possible, the corral or paddock should be nearby.

Flexibility.—Possible changes in use make it desirable for horse barns to be as flexible as possible, even to the point that they can be cheaply and easily converted into cabins, garages, storage buildings, or buildings for other uses. Also, for suburbanites and renters, permanent, portable barns are advantageous.

Materials

When building materials for horse barns are bought, the factors to be considered are initial cost, durability and maintenance, attractiveness, and fire resistance.

Some of the materials available and being used are wood, including plywood; metal; masonry, including concrete, concrete block, cinder, pumice block, brick, and stone; and plastics. Also, preengineered and prefabricated horse barns are being used more often, especially on smaller horse establishments.

Building plans for a small horse barn are shown in figure 57. Complete working drawings may be obtained through county agricultural agents or from extension agricultural engineers at most State agricultural colleges. There is usually a small charge. When asking for working drawings, specify Plan No. 5838, "Riding Horse Barn."

If working drawings of this plan are not available in your State, write to the U.S. Department of Agriculture, Agricultural Engineering Research Division, Plant Industry Station, Beltsville, Md. 20705. The U.S. Department of Agriculture does not distribute drawings but will direct you to a State that does distribute them.

Feed and Water Equipment

The design of feed and water equipment should fill the basic need for simple and effective equipment with which to provide hay, concentrates, minerals, and water without waste or hazard to the horse. Whenever possible, for convenience and safety, feed and water equipment should be located so it can be filled without the caretaker entering the stall or corral.

Feed and water equipment may be built-in or

detached. Because specialty feed and water equipment is more sanitary, flexible, and suitable, many horsemen favor it over old-style wood mangers and concrete or steel tanks. Bulk-tank feed storage may be used to advantage on large horse establishments to eliminate sacks, lessen rodent and bird problems, and make it possible to obtain feed at lower prices by ordering large amounts.

The kind, size, and location of the most common equipment used to hold concentrates, hay, minerals, and water are as follows:

Concentrates.—Pail, tub, or box.

(1) A pail or tub can be made of metal, plastic, or rubber. Usually it has screw eyes and hooks or snaps so it can be suspended. The capacity should be 16 to 20 quarts for horses and 14 to 16 quarts for ponies.

In a stall, the pail or tub should be at the front of the stall. The height should be two-thirds the height of the animal at the withers, or 38 to 42 inches for horses and 28 to 32 inches for ponies.

In a corral, put the tub or pail along a fence line and at the same height as in a stall.

For sanitary reasons removable concentrate containers are preferable so they can be easily and frequently cleaned. This is especially important after feeding a wet mash.

(2) A wooden box for horses should be 12 to 16 inches wide, 24 to 30 inches long, and 8 to 10 inches deep. A box for ponies should be 10 to 12 inches wide, 20 to 24 inches long, and 6 to 8 inches deep.

The location and height of a box in a stall are the same as for a pail or tub. Do not use a wooden box in a corral.

If desired, a wedge-shaped metal pan set on a wooden shelf can be mounted in a front corner of the stall and pivoted so it can be pulled out for filling and cleaning and then pushed back into the stall and locked in place.

Hay.—Stall rack, manger, or corral rack.

(1) A stall rack may be made of metal, fiber, or plastic. A rack for horses should hold 25 to 30 pounds of hay and a rack for ponies, 10 to 15 pounds. It should be in a corner of the stall. The bottom of the rack should be the same height as the horse or pony at the withers.

Hayracks lessen hay contamination, para-sitic infestation, pawing by horses, and hay waste. Racks should open at the bottom so dirt, chaff, and trash may be removed or allowed to fall out. For stallions and broodmares, use high racks to lessen injury hazards.

(2) A wooden manger may be used. It should be 30 inches wide and 24 to 30 inches long for horses and 20 inches square for ponies. Put the manger in the front or in a corner of the stall. The height should be 30 to 42 inches for horses and 20 to 24 inches for ponies.

(3) A corral rack is made of wood. It should be large enough to hold a 1-day supply of hay for the intended number of horses. Put the rack in the fence line of the corral if horses feed from one side only. Put it on high ground if horses feed from both sides.

The top of the rack may be 1 to 2 feet higher than the horses at the withers. Corral hay racks that feed from both sides should be portable.

Minerals.—Box or self-feeder.

A box may be made of wood and a self-feeder may be made of metal or wood. In a stall, the box or self-feeder should be in a corner of the stall and should be the same height as the box or pail used for concentrates.

In a corral, mineral containers should be in a fence corner. The height should be two-thirds the height of the horse at the withers. If a mineral container is in the open, it should be protected from wind and rain. Mineral containers should have two compartments, one for mineral mix and the other for salt.

Water.—Automatic stall waterer, automatic corral waterer, pail, or tank.

(1) Automatic waterers are made of metal. Waterers should be located in a front corner of a stall or in a fence corner of a corral or pasture.

Watering equipment should be designed to facilitate draining and cleaning. Locate waterers a considerable distance from feed containers if possible. Otherwise, horses will carry feed to the waterer or drip water in the concentrate container. A large 20- by 30-inch automatic waterer will accommodate about 25 horses; a two-cup waterer, about 12.

The daily water requirements for horses are: Mature horse, 12 gallons; foal to 2-year-old, and pony, 6 to 8 gallons. In cold areas, waterers should be heated and equipped with thermostatic controls. A satisfactory water temperature range in winter is 40° to 45° F. and in summer 60° to 75°.

Check automatic waterers daily.

(2) A water pail may be made of metal, plastic, or rubber. It should be located in the front of the stall. The height should be two-thirds the height of the horse at the withers, or 38 to 42 inches for horses and 28 to 32 inches for ponies.

(3) A water tank may be concrete or steel. It is used in a corral and should be set in the fence so there are no protruding corners. If it is out in a corral or pasture away from a fence, it should be painted white so the horses can see it at night.

A tank should be 30 by 36 inches high. Allow 1 linear foot of tank space to each five horses. A tank should be equipped with a float valve that is protected from the horses.

Fences for Horses

Good fences (1) maintain boundaries, (2) make horse training and other operations possible, (3) reduce losses to both animals and crops, (4) increase property values, (5) promote better relationships between neighbors, (6) lessen the likelihood of car accidents from animals getting on roads, and (7) add to the attractiveness and distinctiveness of the premises.

Large pastures in which the concentration of horses is not too great may be fenced with woven wire. The mesh of the woven wire fence should be small so horses cannot get their feet through it. Corrals, paddocks, and small pastures require stronger materials. The deficiencies of board and pole fences are: They must be kept painted; they splinter, break, and rot; and they are chewed by horses.

Until recently, conventional metal fences of steel, aluminum, wrought iron, chain link, or cable had one or more deficiencies. But metal fences have greatly improved in recent years.

Table 6 lists the materials and specifications commonly used for horse fences.

Show-Rings

Show-rings have no standard or required specifications for ring size, type of construction, or maintenance.

For most purposes, a ring 125 x 250 feet will suffice. However, many good show-rings are either smaller or larger than this. For example, the ring of the famous Devon Horse Show, which is often used for jumpers, is 150 x 300 feet. But the ring at the Spanish Riding School in Vienna is only 59 x 180 feet.

TABLE 6.—*Horse fences*

Post and fencing material	Post length and diameter	Size of rails, boards, or poles and gage of wire	Fence height	Number of rails, boards, or poles and mesh of wire	Distance between posts on centers
			Inches		Feet
Steel or aluminum posts and rails.[1]	7½ ft	10 or 20 ft. long	60	3 rails	10
	7½ ft	10 or 20 ft. long	60	4 rails	10
	8½ ft	10 or 20 ft. long	72	4 rails	10
Wooden posts and boards.	7½ ft.; 4 to 8 in	2 x 6 or 2 x 8 in. boards	60	4 boards	8
	8½ ft.; 4 to 8 in	2 x 6 or 2 x 8 in. boards	72	5 boards	8
Wooden posts and poles.	7½ ft.; 4 to 8 in	4 to 6 in. diameter	60	4 poles	8
	8½ ft.; 4 to 8 in	4 to 6 in. diameter	72	5 poles	8
Wooden posts and woven wire.[2]	7½ ft.; 4 to 8 in	9 or 11 gage staywire	55 to 58	12-in. mesh	12

[1] Because of the strength of most metal, fewer rails and posts are necessary than when wood is used.
[2] Use 1 or 2 strands of barbed wire—with barbs 3 to 4 inches apart—on top of the fence.

The surface of a show-ring must be resilient and firm to assure proper footing, and it also must be free of dust. In outdoor rings, proper drainage and a good track base are necessary for all-weather use. A ring can be drained by (1) locating it high enough for water to drain away from it and (2) when necessary, installing drainage tile or perforated steel pipe underneath the track, with the perforations on the bottom side of the pipe.

The track usually will be firm if it is covered with a mixture of organic matter and dirt or sand. For example, the ring at the Spanish Riding School is covered with a mixture of two-thirds sawdust and one-third sand. It is sprinkled with water at intervals to keep down the dust.

In many indoor rings in the United States, 6 to 8 inches of tanbark are used on a dirt base. Unless tanbark is watered frequently, it will pulverize and give poor footing. Some rings are covered 18 to 24 inches deep with shavings or sawdust mixed with dirt or sand. Other rings are covered with approximately 9 inches of wood shavings, 2 inches of sawdust, and 4 inches of sand all mixed together and oiled. Salt may be added because it holds moisture when wetted down and reduces dust.

In outdoor rings, organic matter for resilience is sometimes provided by seeding rye or other small grain on the track during the off-season and disking under the green crop.

No matter how good the construction, a show-ring must be maintained. It must be smoothed and leveled, holes must be filled, and when it gets too hard, the ground must be broken. A flexible, chain-type harrow is recommended for show-ring maintenance.

Besides ring size, construction, and maintenance, other factors to be considered are (1) ring layout to facilitate reversing a performance class in a ring that has turf or other decorative material in the center; (2) attractiveness of the ring; (3) spectator seating capacity, comfort, and visibility; (4) nearby parking; and (5) handling the crowd.

DISEASES AND PARASITES

Horse owners and caretakers have a responsibility for the horses in their care. They must protect their animals from diseases and parasites. *The information given here on diseases and parasites is intended only as a guide for horse owners. It is not intended to be used in lieu of the services of a veterinarian.* At the first sign of illness in their horses, owners should call a veterinarian for diagnosis and treatment.

General Health Program

A strict program of sanitation, disease prevention, and parasite control is necessary to protect the health of horses. Although the exact program will vary from farm to farm, the basic principles are the same. A horseman may compare the following general program with his existing program and use it to develop similar and more specific programs.

(1) Avoid public feeding and watering facilities.

(2) Read the sections in this handbook that discuss the diseases and parasites of horses; become familiar with symptoms and treatments.

(3) When signs of infectious disease appear, isolate affected animals promptly, provide them with separate water and feed containers, and *follow the instructions and prescribed treatment of a veterinarian.*

(4) Prevent or control parasites by adhering to the following program:

   (a) Provide good sanitation and a high level of nutrition.

   (b) Have adequate acreage. Use temporary seeded pasture rather than permanent pasture, and practice rotation grazing.

   (c) Pasture young animals on clean pastures. Never allow them to graze on an infested area unless the area has been either plowed or left idle for a year.

   (d) Do not spread fresh horse manure on pastures grazed by horses. Either store the manure in a suitable pit for at least 2 weeks or spread it on fields that are to be plowed and cropped.

(e) When small pastures or paddocks must be used, pick up droppings at frequent intervals.

(f) Keep pastures mowed and harrowed. Use a chain harrow.

(g) Prevent fecal contamination of feed and water.

(h) Administer suitable vermifuges when internal parasites are present. The choice of vermifuges and administration of them should be by a veterinarian. Later move horses to a clean area.

(i) Apply the proper insecticide when external parasites are present.

(j) If cattle are on the farm, alternate the use of pastures between cattle and horses because horse parasites die in cattle.

(k) Avoid overgrazing because more parasites are present on the bottom inch of grass.

(l) As a disease preventive measure, arrange a scheduled yearly vaccination program with your veterinarian.

Health Program for Breeding and Foaling

(1) Mate only healthy mares to healthy stallions and observe scrupulous cleanliness at the time of service and examination. Never breed a mare that has any kind of discharge.

(2) Provide plenty of exercise for the stallion and pregnant mare in harness, under saddle, or by turning them loose in a large pasture where plenty of shade and water are available.

(3) During spring and fall when the weather is warm, allow the mare to foal in a clean, open pasture away from other livestock. During bad weather, keep the mare in a roomy, well-lighted, well-ventilated box stall that is provided with clean bedding. Before using the stall, thoroughly disinfect it with a lye solution made by adding one can of lye to 12 to 15

gallons of water. After the foal is born, remove all wet, stained, or soiled bedding and dust the floor lightly with lime. Do not use too much lime because it irritates the eyes and nasal passages of foals. When the afterbirth has been completely discharged, it should be buried in lime or burned. The mare should be kept isolated until all discharges have stopped.

(4) To lessen the danger of navel infection, promptly treat the navel cord of the newborn foal with tincture of iodine.

(5) As a precaution against foaling diseases and other infections, a veterinarian may administer antibiotics to both the mare and foal on the day of foaling.

Health Program for New Horses and Visiting Mares

(1) Isolate new animals for 3 weeks before adding them to the herd. During this period, a veterinarian may administer sleeping sickness vaccine in season and tetanus toxoid, make a thorough general and parasitic examination, make a genital examination of breeding animals, and treat animals when necessary.

(2) Make sure that mares brought in for breeding are accompanied by a health certificate issued by a veterinarian. Closely watch mares that have had trouble foaling or have lost foals.

(3) If possible, saddle, bridle, or harness visiting mares near their own isolation quarters and use tack and equipment that is not used by mares kept on the establishment.

Diseases of Horses

The following summary of diseases is intended only to supplement the services of a veterinarian to help provide more rapid detection of trouble, and to improve nursing care for sick horses.

(1) **Anthrax** (splenic fever, charbon).—An acute, infectious disease caused by *Bacillus anthracis*, a large, rod-shaped organism.

Symptoms.—This disease has a history of sudden deaths. Sick animals are feverish, excitable, and later depressed. They carry the head low, lag behind the herd, and breathe rapidly. Swellings appear over the body and around the neck region. Milk secretion may turn bloody or stop entirely, and there may be a bloody discharge from all body openings.

Treatment.—Isolate all sick animals. At the first sign of any of the above symptoms, a veterinarian should be called at once. The veterinarian may give large quantities of antibiotic (3 to 12 million units of penicillin). In the early stages of the disease, 50 to 100 milliliters (ml.) of antianthrax serum may also be helpful. Provide good nursing care.

Control.—Quarantine infected herds. All carcasses and contaminated material should be burned completely or buried deeply and covered with quicklime, preferably on the spot. Vaccinate all exposed but healthy animals, rotate pastures, and initiate a rigid sanitation program. Spray sick and healthy animals with an insecticide to avoid fly transmission of the infection.

Prevention.—In infected areas, vaccination should be repeated each year, usually in the spring. Provide fly control by spraying animals during the insect season.

Discussion.—The disease is general throughout the world in so-called anthrax districts. Cattle are more susceptible to anthrax than horses. A farmer or rancher should never open the carcass of a dead animal suspected of having died from anthrax. Instead, a veterinarian should be summoned at the first sign of an outbreak. Control measures should be carried out under the supervision of a veterinarian. The bacillus that causes anthrax can survive for years in a spore stage, resisting all destructive agents.

(2) Distemper (strangles).—A widespread contagious disease caused by *Streptococcus equi*, a bacterium.

Symptoms.—Sick animals show depression, loss of appetite, high fever, and a discharge from the nose. By the third or fourth day of the disease, the glands under the jaw start to enlarge, become sensitive, and eventually break open and discharge pus. A cough is present.

Treatment.—Good nursing is the most important treatment. This includes clean, fresh water, good feed, uniform temperature, and shelter away from drafts. A veterinarian may prescribe one of the sulfas or antibiotics, or both.

Control.—Put affected animals in strict quarantine. Clean and disinfect contaminated quarters and premises.

Prevention.—Prevention consists of avoiding contact with infected animals or contaminated feeds, premises, and equipment. The injection of animals with bacterin containing killed *Streptococcus equi* will help raise the level of immunity and may prevent the disease. However, the use of bacterins is not always beneficial.

Discussion.—The disease is worldwide and it attacks animals of any age, but it is most common in young stock. Death losses are low. Affected animals are usually immune for the remainder of life.

(3) Encephalomyelitis (sleeping sickness).—A virus, epizootic (epidemic) disease that may be carried by birds and mosquitoes. It is caused by four different viruses. The two most common ones are known as the eastern type and the western type.

Symptoms.—In early stages, animals walk aimlessly about, crashing into objects. Later they may appear sleepy and stand with a lowered head. Grinding of the teeth, inability to swallow, paralysis of the lips, and blindness may be noted. Paralysis may cause animals to fall. If affected animals do not recover, death occurs in 2 to 4 days.

Treatment.—Careful nursing is perhaps the most important treatment. Serum treatment is sometimes effective when given very early in the disease. A veterinarian should be consulted about this.

Control.—Control measures include prompt disposal of all infected carcasses; destruction, if possible, of insect breeding grounds; and as little movement as possible of animals from an epizootic area to a clean one.

Prevention.—Vaccinate all animals before May of each year or as soon as the disease makes its appearance in a community.

Discussion.—The disease is widespread. Since 1930, nearly a million horses and mules have been affected in the United States. Some animals make full recovery but other survivors do not. The mortality rate in the western type is about 30 percent, but in the eastern type it is 90 percent or higher. Birds and wild rodents are natural disease hosts for the western type. Mosquitoes (*Culex tarsalis*) transmit the disease.

(4) **Equine abortion** (premature expulsion of the fetus).—The causes of abortion may be grouped under five headings as follows:

(a) *Salmonella abortivoequina* abortion occurs most frequently in the last half of pregnancy.

(b) Streptococcic abortion usually occurs early in pregnancy—prior to the fifth month.

(c) Virus, or epizootic abortion (rhinopneumonitis), generally occurs late in pregnancy—after the fifth month. Some foals are born alive and die at 2 to 3 days of age.

(d) Viral arteritis is caused by a virus. It produces fever, inflammation of the mucosa in the respiratory tract, and edema of the eyelids and legs. As many as 50 to 80 percent of pregnant mares may abort.

(e) Miscellaneous causes of abortion may be due to such things as accidents, faulty feeds, or twins.

Treatment.—Quarantine animals that have aborted and give them good feed and care.

Control.—Burn or bury the bedding and fetus of mares that have aborted. Disinfect contaminated premises. Isolate newly introduced animals to the farm.

Prevention.—Prevent abortion caused by *Salmonella abortivoequina* by vaccinating all pregnant mares with a bacterin every year where premises are infected with the organism.

Prevent streptococcic abortion by mating only healthy animals and observing scrupulous cleanliness at mating.

Prevent rhinopneumonitis by intranasal inoculation with hamster-adapted virus. Inoculate all horses of both sexes and all ages in July and October of each year.

Prevent viral arteritis by isolating new horses to the farm and quarantining affected animals. No vaccines are available for immunization.

VEE

In 1971, an outbreak of Venezuelan Equine Encephalomyelitis (VEE) was reported in Texas. This was the first time the disease had occurred in the United States.

VEE is an infectious virus disease of the central nervous system of horses, causing mortality as high as 80 to 90 percent. The disease also may attack humans. The symptoms of VEE in horses are similar to those in the common eastern and western types of encephalomyelitis. In humans the infection usually produces a mild to severe respiratory illness with severe frontal headache and high fever. Children usually are affected more severely than adults. VEE is generally not fatal in humans but some deaths have been reported.

VEE was first diagnosed in Venezuela in 1936 and was reported in several South and Central American countries before the outbreak occurred in the United States.

VEE is transmitted by mosquitoes and other insects. There is also a possibility of contact transmission between horses. Rodents are susceptible to VEE and they may be reservoirs of the virus in the natural spread of the disease.

In 1971, a program to control the spread of VEE was initiated. It included spraying to control mosquitoes and the vaccination of horses.

Discussion.—It is estimated that for the United States as a whole, one-half of all pregnant mares either abort or produce weak foals. Sanitation and herd health are important factors in lessening the number of abortions regardless of kind. *Consult a veterinarian* whenever abortion occurs. Cattle abortion on the premises will not affect pregnant mares and cause them to abort.

(5) **Equine infectious anemia** (swamp fever).—An infectious virus disease.

Symptoms.—Symptoms of the disease vary, but usually they include some of the following: high and intermittent fever; depression; stiffness and weakness, especially in the hindquarters; anemia; jaundice; edema and swelling of the lower body and legs; unthriftiness; and loss of condition and weight, even though the appetite is good. Most affected animals die within 2 to 4 weeks.

Treatment.—No successful treatment is known.

Control.—Segregate infected animals and have them use separate feeding and watering facilities. Kill sick animals and burn or bury their carcasses.

Prevention.—Use disposable hypodermic needles when horses are vaccinated against disease and sterilize all other skin penetrating instruments by boiling them at least 15 minutes after each use. Practice good sanitation and eliminate or reduce biting insects as much as possible. Watch for sick horses and get a diagnosis by a veterinarian if any are observed. Use separate tack equipment on each horse. Keep stalls, starting gates, and other facilities clean at racetracks and shows. This disease has existed in different sections of the United States for at least 50 years but no preventive vaccination is known.

Discussion.—Infected horses may be virus carriers for years and are a danger to susceptible horses.

(6) **Equine influenza.**—An infectious disease caused by a myxovirus that has properties of the Type A influenza viruses.

Symptoms.—Young animals, except for very young foals that have immunity from the dam's milk, are particularly susceptible. Older animals are usually immune. Symptoms develop 2 to 10 days after exposure. The onset of the disease is marked by a rapidly rising temperature that may reach 106° F. and persist for 2 to 10 days. Other symptoms include loss of appetite, extreme weakness and depression, rapid breathing, a dry cough, and a watery discharge from the eyes and nostrils that is followed by a white to yellow nasal discharge.

Treatment.—Treatment should be handled by a veterinarian. Avoid exercising the animals during the period of elevated temperature. The use of antibiotics and/or sulfa drugs may prevent some of the complicated secondary conditions.

Control.—Avoid transmission of the virus on contaminated feed, bedding, water, buckets, brooms, clothing and hands of attendants, and transportation facilities.

Prevention.—Vaccinate with a killed virus. Use two doses; follow the manufacturer's directions on the time of the second dose. Also, give each animal an annual booster shot, or a booster when animals are exposed or when an epidemic occurs. Quarantine sick animals, and isolate all new animals to the premises for 3 weeks.

Discussion.—The disease is widespread throughout the world. It frequently appears where a number of horses are assembled, such as racetracks, sales, and shows. The death rate is low but economic loss is high. The disease interrupts training, racing, and showing schedules and it may force the withdrawal of animals from sales. Although horses, swine, and humans are subject to influenza and the symptoms are similar for each, there appears to be no transmission of the disease between any of them.

(7) **Glanders** (farcy).—An acute or chronic infectious disease caused by *Malleomyces mallei*, a bacterium.

Symptoms.—The chronic form most often attacks horses, affecting the lungs, skin, or nasal passages. There may be a nasal discharge that later becomes pus, and nodules and ulcers may appear in the skin. With the lung type, there generally is loss in condition, lack of endurance, bleeding and a mucus discharge from the nose, and coughing. The skin of the extremities may develop ulcers that exude a honeylike tenacious discharge.

The acute form more often attacks mules and donkeys. The symptoms are similar to the chronic form, but more severe. Death usually occurs in a week.

Treatment.—No cure is known.

Control.—Use the mallein test to detect infected animals or animals suspected of having the disease. Destroy infected animals and clean and disinfect contaminated equipment and premises.

Prevention.—Avoid inhalation or ingestion of the causative organism. Do not use public watering places.

Discussion.—Glanders is prevalent in areas where horses still are used for transportation and work. The disease has largely disappeared from the mechanized areas of the world, including the United States, but it is not eradicated. Through the transport of animals, glanders can make its appearance anytime in any area.

(8) **Naval infection** (joint ill, navel ill, actinobaccillosis, streptococcus). An infectious disease of newborn animals caused by several kinds of bacteria.

Symptoms.—Infected animals have loss of appetite; swelling, soreness, and stiffness in the joints; general listlessness; and umbilical swelling and discharge.

Treatment.—A veterinarian may give a blood transfusion from the dam to the offspring, or he may administer a sulfa, an antibiotic, a serum, or a bacterin.

Control.—See prevention.

Prevention.—Practice good sanitation and hygiene at mating and parturition. Feed iodized salt to pregnant mares in iodine-deficient areas. Soon after birth, treat the navel cord of newborn animals with tincture of iodine.

Discussion.—The disease appears throughout the United States. About 50 percent of infected foals die and many that survive have deformed joints. Providing clean quarters for the newborn and painting the navel cord with tincture of iodine are the best preventive measures.

(9) **Tetanus** (lockjaw).—Chiefly a wound-infection disease caused by a powerful toxin, more than 100 times as toxic as strychnine, that is liberated by the bacterium *Clostridium tetani*, an anaerobe.

Symptoms.—This disease usually is associated with a wound. First sign of tetanus is a stiffness about the head. Animals often chew slowly and weakly and swallow awkwardly. The third or inner eyelid protrudes over the forward surface of the eyeball. The slightest noise or movement causes sick animals to have violent spasms. Usually sick animals remain standing until close to death. All ages are susceptible.

Treatment.—Place sick animals under the care of a veterinarian and keep them quiet. Good nursing is important. If given early in the disease, massive doses of antitoxin, 100,000 to 200,000 units or more, may be effective. Also, tranquilizers will reduce the extent and severity of muscular spasms, and antibiotics will help.

Control.—See prevention.

Prevention.—Under the direction of a veterinarian, give tetanus toxoid in two doses at 6-week intervals, followed by a booster injection annually. If premises are unsanitary, all surgery should be accompanied with tetanus antitoxin.

Discussion.—Tetanus is worldwide, but in the United States it occurs most frequently in the South. Death occurs in over half of the affected cases.

(10) **Vesicular stomatitis.**—A contagious disease of the mouth caused by a virus.

Symptoms.—Blisters and rawness appear mainly on the tongue but also on the inner surfaces of the lips, angles of the mouth, and the gums. There is considerable salivation. Symptoms appear in 2 to 5 days after exposure.

Treatment.—Make the animal as comfortable as possible and provide plenty of water and soft feed.

Control.—None.

Prevention.—None. No vaccination is available.

Discussion.—The disease may affect 50 percent of the animals on the premises.

Parasites of Horses [7]

Parasites live in or on the bodies of host animals. Parasites kill some horses but the main damage is lowered efficiency. Attacks are insidious and cause damage before it is noticed.

Internal parasites

Some 150 different kinds of internal parasites attack horses throughout the world and probably no animal is ever entirely free of them. Parasites may be located in practically every tissue and cavity of the body. However, most of

---

[7] Trade names of pesticides used to control parasites are mentioned in this publication solely to provide specific information. Mention of a trade name does not constitute a guarantee of the product by the U.S. Department of Agriculture nor does it imply an endorsement by the Department over comparable products that are not named. When any trade-named compound is used, the directions for use given on the label should be followed very carefully.

them are in the alimentary tract, lungs, body cavity, or bloodstream. Those in the digestive system usually become localized there, but others travel throughout different parts of the body.

The general symptoms of parasitic infection in horses are weakness, unthriftiness, emaciation, tucked-up flanks, distended abdomen, rough coat, pale membranes in the eyes and mouth, stunted growth in young animals, and in some cases frequent colic and diarrhea. Affected animals usually eat well and the temperature remains normal. But an infected animal always loses some efficiency as a working unit.

Few treatments with only one drug are effective in removing bots and various gastrointestinal worms from horses. Usually, it is necessary to use a combination of drugs. For this purpose, the specific combination is dependent upon the kinds of parasites present in the horses to be treated. *It is always wise, therefore, to obtain a definite diagnosis from a veterinarian or veterinary diagnostic laboratory before treatment is given.* A veterinarian should always be consulted for safe and effective dosages of the various drugs and treatment schedules.

The common internal parasites of horses and some of the drugs used to treat them are as follows:

Parasites in the stomach

(1) **Stomach worms** (*Habronema* spp., *Trichostrongylus axei*).—A group of parasitic worms that produces inflammation of the stomach.

Symptoms.—Horses suffer loss of condition and severe gastritis. Sometimes, the larvae of large stomach worms are partially responsible for the skin disease of horses called summer sores.

Treatment.—Probably the best drug to use for *Habronema* spp. is carbon disulfide. Dosage and administration should be determined by a veterinarian. No drugs have been tested adequately against *Trichostrongylus axei*, the small stomach worm.

Prevention and control.—Provide good sanitation, proper manure disposal, and fly control.

Discussion.—Stomach worms attack horses throughout the United States. Wasted feed and lowered efficiency are the chief losses.

(2) **Bots** (*Gasterophilus* spp.).—Four species of bots have been found in the United States but only three are serious pests of horses.

Symptoms.—Animals attacked by the botfly may toss their heads in the air, strike the ground with their front feet, and rub their noses on each other or any convenient object. Animals infected with bots may show frequent digestive upsets and even colic, lowered vitality and emaciation, and reduced work output. Bots may penetrate the stomach wall and cause death.

Treatment.—Use of carbon disulfide, trichlorfon, or dichlorvos under the direction of a veterinarian is recommended.

Prevention and control.—Frequent grooming, washing, and clipping help prevent bot attacks. Prevention of reinfection is best assured through community campaigns in which all horses within the area are treated. Fly nets and nose covers offer some relief from the attacks of botflies.

Discussion.—Bots are worldwide. The presence of bots results in loss of feed to feeding worms, itching and loss of tail hair from rubbing, lowered work efficiency, retarded growth of young animals, lowered breeding efficiency, and death in severe infections.

Parasites in the small intestine

(1) **Large roundworms or ascarids** (*Parascaris equorum*).—The female varies from 6 to 22 inches long and the male from 5 to 13 inches. When full grown, both are about the diameter of a lead pencil.

Symptoms.—The injury caused by ascarids ranges from light infections producing moderate effects to heavy infections that may cause death. Death usually is due to a ruptured intestine. Serious lung damage caused by migrating ascarid larvae may result in pneumonia. More common are retarded growth and development manifested by a potbelly, rough hair coat, and digestive disturbances. Ascarids affect foals and young animals, but rarely affect horses over 5 years old; older animals develop immunity from early infections.

Treatment.—Veterinarians most commonly use one of the following compounds for the treatment of this parasite: carbon disulfide, piperazine compounds, trichlorfon, dichlorvos, or thiabendazole.

Prevention and control.—Keep the foaling barn and paddocks clean, store manure in a pit 2 to 3 weeks, provide clean feed and water, and place young foals on clean pasture.

Discussion.—Ascarids attack horses throughout the United States. The presence of ascarids results in loss of feed to feeding worms, lowered work efficiency, retarded growth in young animals, lowered breeding efficiency, and death in severe infections.

(2) Threadworm (*Strongyloides westeri*).—Threadworms are also known as strongyloides.

Symptoms.—Threadworms attack foals, causing diarrhea. The worms disappear by the time foals are 6 months old.

Prevention and control.—Provide good sanitation and clean, dry bedding.

Discussion.— These worms are common where there is a concentration of foals. Losses are primarily in stunted growth and unthriftiness.

(3) Tapeworms (*Anoplocephala magna, A. perfoliata, Paranoplocephala mamillana*).—*Anoplocephala perfoliata* is the most common and most damaging.

Symptoms.—Heavy infections may cause digestive disturbances, loss in weight, and anemia.

Treatment.—Traditional treatments are areca nut, kamala, and oleoresin of male fern; no modern effective drugs have been developed for treatment of tapeworm infections in horses.

Prevention and control.—Provide good sanitation and husbandry, proper manure disposal, and clean bedding.

Discussion.—Tapeworms attack horses throughout the northern part of the United States. Losses are primarily in wasted feed and retarded growth.

Parasites in the large intestine

(1) **Large and small strongyles** (*Strongylus*

spp. and others).—There are about 60 species of strongyles. Three are large worms that grow up to 2 inches long. The rest are small and some are barely visible to the eye. Large strongyles are variously called bloodworms (*Strongylus vulgaris*), palisade worms, sclerostomes, and red worms.

Symptoms.—Infected horses have lack of appetite, anemia, progressive emaciation, a rough hair coat, sunken eyes, digestive disturbances including colic, a tucked-up appearance, and sometimes posterior paralysis and death. Collectively these symptoms indicate the disease known as strongylosis. Harmful effects are greatest in young animals. One species of large strongyles (*Strongylus vulgaris*) may permanently damage the intestinal blood vessel wall and cause death at any age.

Treatment.—Use thiabendazole; phenothiazine + piperazine; phenothiazine + piperazine-1-carbodithioic acid; dithiazanine + piperazine; trichlorfon; or dichlorvos. The decision as to which drugs to use and the dosage level should be made by a veterinarian.

Prevention and control.—Gather manure daily from pastures and barns and store it in a pit 2 to 3 weeks. Rotate pastures and avoid moist pasture and overstocking.

Discussion.—Strongyles attack horses throughout the United States wherever horses are pastured. Attacks of strongyles result in loss of feed to feeding worms, lowered work efficiency, retarded growth of young animals, lowered breeding efficiency, and death in severe infections.

(2) **Pinworms** (*Oxyuris equi, Probstmyria vivipara*).—Two species of pinworms, or rectal worms, frequently are found in horses. *Oxyuris equi* are whitish worms with long, slender tails. *Probstmyria vivipara* are so small they are scarcely visible to the eye.

Symptoms.—The symptoms are irritation of the anus and tail rubbing. Heavy infections also may cause digestive disturbances and anemia. Large pinworms are most damaging to horses and may be seen in the feces of heavily infected animals.

Treatment.—The common drugs are thiabendazole, trichlorfon, or dichlorvos or various combinations of trichlorfon, phenothiazine, piperazine, and thiabendazole. Which drugs to give and dosage should be determined by a veterinarian.

Prevention and control.—Provide good sanitation and keep animals separated from their own excrement.

Discussion.—Pinworms attack horses throughout the United States.

Parasites in the lungs

(1) **Lungworms** (*Dictyocaulus arnfieldi*).— The equine lungworm is very rare in the United States.

Symptoms.—Donkeys seem to be able to carry large numbers of lungworms without showing any symptoms. They develop a tolerance. However, infected foals may become unthrifty and develop a cough. There is a rise in temperature with lungworm infection.

Prevention and control.—Where lungworm infection is suspected, a fecal examination should be made. Infected burros should be kept away from foals.

Discussion.—Lungworms may be found in the air passages of the horse and other equines. The male worm reaches a length of about 1 inch and the female may be about 2 inches long. The eggs are laid in the lungs and pass out of the horse's body through the intestine. They hatch into first-stage larvae that develop eventually into the third, or infective, stage. The infective larvae enter the body through the mouth, travel in the lymph vessels to the thoracic duct, then to the heart, and eventually to the lungs.

Blood protozoan parasites

(1) **Equine piroplasmosis** (babesiasis).— Caused by *Babesia caballi* or *B. equi*, protozoan parasites that invade the red blood cells.

Symptoms.—Equine piroplasmosis is similar to equine infectious anemia but a positive diagnosis can be made by determining whether or not protozoa are in the red blood cells. Symptoms include a fever of 103° to 106° F., anemia, jaundice, depression, thirst, a discharge from the eyes, and swelling of the eyelids. Constipation and colic may occur and the urine is a yellow to reddish color. Symptoms appear 1 to 3 weeks after exposure.

Treatment.—A number of treatments are used but the choice should be left to a veterinarian. Many States have laws that require you to report this infection.

Prevention and control.— Control the ticks that carry the parasites, especially brown dog ticks and tropical horse ticks, both of which are found in the United States. Methods of tick control are discussed in the section on external parasites. Practice rigid sanitation in the use of all syringes, needles, and medical instruments. Recovered animals remain carriers for 10 months to 4 years and should be isolated.

Discussion.—This infection is worldwide. In the United States, it was first diagnosed in Florida in 1961. The death rate is from 10 to 15 percent of infected animals.

External parasites

Several kinds of external parasites attack horses. These pests lower the vitality of horses, damage the hair and skin, and produce a generally unthrifty condition.

External parasites also are responsible for the spread of several serious diseases of horses. Equine piroplasmosis (babesiasis) is transmitted by a tick, *Dermacentor nitens*. Mosquitoes (Culicidae) are vectors of equine infectious anemia (swamp fever) and equine encephalomyelitis (sleeping sickness).

The common measures used to prevent and control external parasites of horses are practicing good sanitation, good grooming, avoiding a too heavy concentration of horses, and spraying or dusting with insecticides. Flies and lice are the most common external parasites of horses but some of the others can produce more severe injury when they occur.

The common external parasites of horses and approved control measures are as follows:

(1) **Blowfly.**—The blowfly group consists of several species of flies that breed in animal flesh.

Symptoms.—The maggots of blowflies infest wounds and spread over the body, feeding on the skin surface, producing severe irritation, and destroying the ability of the skin to function. Infested animals rapidly become weak, fevered, and unthrifty.

Treatment.—A 0.25 percent coumaphos (Co-Ral) spray is effective for controlling blowfly larvae infesting soiled hair and wounds.

Prevention and control.—To control the blowfly, destroy dead animals by burning or deep burial and by using traps, poisoned baits, electrified screens, and repellents.

Discussion.—Blowfly attacks are widespread but they present the greatest problem in the Pacific Northwest, the South, and the Southwest. Death losses are not large but work efficiency is lowered.

(2) **House fly and stable fly.**—House flies are nonbiting, nuisance insects. Stable flies are biting insects that bite principally on the legs.

Symptoms.— Flies annoy horses, causing them to fight. Horses may strike the ground with their feet, toss their heads, switch their tails, and run.

Treatment.—Treat animals infested with house and stable flies with any of the following insecticides, using the dosages given. Indication is shown if the treatment is also effective against horn flies.

Carbaryl spray, 0.5 percent, 1 quart, not more often than every 4 days. (Also for horn flies.)

Ciodrin spray, 0.15 to 0.3 percent, 1 quart, not more often than every 7 days. (Also for horn flies.)

Ciodrin mist spray, 2 percent in oil, 1 to 2 ounces. (Mist spray is composed of very fine, or minute, droplets.)

Coumaphos spray, 0.06 to 0.25 percent, 1 to 2 quarts, to backs of animals every 3 weeks or as needed. (Also for horn flies.)

Dioxathion spray, 0.15 percent, 1 to 2 quarts, not more often than once every 2 weeks. (Also for horn flies.)

Dichlorvos mist spray, 1 percent in oil, 1 to 2 ounces. (Also for horn flies.)

Malathion spray, 0.5 percent, 2 quarts, to backs every 3 weeks or as needed. (Also for horn flies.)

Methoxychlor spray, 0.5 percent, 1 to 2 quarts, to backs every 3 weeks or as needed. (Also for horn flies.)

Ronnel spray, 0.25 to 0.5 percent, 1 to 2 quarts, to backs every 3 weeks or as needed. (Also for horn flies.)

Pyrethrins and synergist, 1 to 2 quarts when used as a wet spray, or 1 to 2 ounces as a mist spray; repeat every 2 to 3 days as needed. (Wet, or saturating, spray should be applied liberally under pressure to wet the hair coat to the skin.)

The following are effective against house flies but not stable flies: (a) Baits consisting of a 0.5 to 2 percent organophosphate toxicant such as dichlorvos, diazinon, malathion, naled, or trichlorfon mixed with a food attractant such as sugar or sirup; or (b) treated cotton cord impregnated with 10 percent parathion or 25 percent diazinon and suspended from the ceiling.

Prevention and control.—Practice good sanitation, including proper disposal of all fly breeding media such as manure and waste feed. Use screens when practical.

Discussion.—*Habronema* spp., a roundworm, is transmitted by house flies. Stable flies can carry anthrax, infectious anemia, and surra.

(3) **Horn fly.**—Horn flies are primarily pests of cattle but they sometimes seriously annoy horses.

Treatment.—Treat infested animals with any of the insecticides recommended for horn flies in the treatment section under "House Fly and Stable Fly."

(4) **Horsefly, deerfly, and mosquito.**—All of these are biting insects. Bites of horseflies and deerflies are painful.

Treatment.—Use repellent sprays containing 0.05 to 0.1 percent pyrethrins, with or without 0.5 to 0.1 percent synergist. Mists or wet sprays of such formulations will lessen the attacks of biting insects for several hours to a full day. Sprays containing 0.3 percent Ciodrin will provide short-time protection from biting flies and mosquitoes, but do not apply more often than every 7 days.

Prevention and control.—The best method of controlling mosquitoes is to provide drainage or landfill in breeding areas.

Discussion.—Mosquitoes transmit equine encephalomyelitis.

(5) **Face fly.**—Face flies gather in large numbers on the faces of horses, especially around the eyes and nose.

Treatment.—Use a 0.3 percent Ciodrin spray or brush the forehead lightly with a sirup bait containing 0.5 percent dichlorvos (Vapona). These two treatments are effective for only a short time and may have to be applied almost daily.

Prevention and control.—Shelters for horses on pastures give some protection.

(6) Lice.—These are small, flattened, wingless insect parasites. Horses are commonly infested by two species of lice; they are the common horse biting louse, *Damalinia equi*, and the horse sucking louse, *Haematopinas asini*.

Symptoms.—Symptoms include intense irritation, restlessness, and loss of condition. There may be severe itching and the animal may be seen scratching, rubbing, and gnawing the skin; scabs may be evident and the hair may be rough, thin, and without luster. Lice are likely to be most plentiful around the root of the tail, on the inside of the thighs, over the fetlock region, and along the neck and shoulders.

Treatment.—Treat infested animals with any of the following insecticides: Spray with 0.5 percent carbaryl but do not treat more often than every 4 days; spray with 0.3 percent Ciodrin but do not treat more often than every 7 days; spray with 0.125 percent coumaphos (Co–Ral); spray with 0.15 percent dioxathion (Delnav), but only at 2-week intervals and do not treat foals; or spray with 0.5 percent malathion but do not treat foals under 1 month old. A second application after an interval of 12 to 14 days may be required. Repeated treatments are rarely necessary to control lice.

Prevention and control.—Because of the close contact of horses during the winter, it is practically impossible to keep them from becoming infested with lice. For effective control, all horses should be treated with insecticides simultaneously at intervals as needed, especially in the fall about the time they are placed in winter quarters.

Discussion.—Lice are widespread. They retard growth, lower work efficiency, and produce unthriftiness. They show up most commonly on neglected animals in winter.

(7) Mites.—These are very small parasites that cause mange (scabies, scab, and itch). The two chief forms of mange are sarcoptic mange caused by burrowing mites and psoroptic mange caused by mites that bite the skin and suck the serum and lymph but do not burrow. Mites also may cause chorioptic mange.

Symptoms.—Symptoms are irritation, itching, and scratching. The skin crusts over and becomes thick, tough, and wrinkled. Mange appears to spread most rapidly during the winter months.

Treatment.—Treat animals with sprays containing (a) 0.25 percent coumaphos, (b) 0.1 to 0.3 percent Ciodrin, or (c) 0.5 percent malathion; give two treatments 10 to 14 days apart. Lime-sulfur and nicotine sprays are effective but they are little used on horses today.

Prevention and control.—Keep healthy horses away from diseased animals or infested premises. Spray infested animals with insecticides and quarantine affected herds.

Discussion.—Mites are widespread. They retard growth, lower work efficiency, and produce unthriftiness. When sarcoptic and psoroptic mange appear, they must be reported to State or Federal animal health agencies. Also, in many States, chorioptic mange must be reported.

(8) Ringworm.—This is a contagious infection of the outer layers of skin caused by an infestation of microscopic fungi.

Symptoms.—Round, scaly areas almost devoid of hair appear mainly in the vicinity of eyes, ears, side of the neck, or root of the tail. Mild itching usually accompanies the infection.

Treatment.—Clip the hair from the infected skin areas. Soften skin crusts with warm soap and water and remove them if desired. Let infected areas dry and then paint them with weak tincture of iodine every 3 days or treat them with a mixture of one part salicylic acid and 10 parts alcohol every 3 days until the infection clears up.

Prevention and control. — Isolate infected animals. Disinfect everything that has been in contact with infected animals, including curry combs and brushes. Practice strict sanitation.

Discussion.—Ringworm attacks horses throughout the United States, primarily as a stable infection. It is unsightly and infected animals may have considerable discomfort, but economic losses are low.

(9) **Screwworm.**—Maggots of the screwworm fly require living flesh of animals on which to feed.

Symptoms.—Symptoms include loss of appetite, unthriftiness, and lowered activity.

Treatment.—Use ronnel smear. Brush or smear the infected area twice the first week and then weekly until healed. A wash containing 0.25 coumaphos also is effective.

Prevention and control.—Area-wide screwworm eradication by sterilizing pupal-stage screwworms with X-rays or gamma rays has been most effective. Try to keep animals from wounding themselves and protect any wounds that do occur. Schedule castrations in winter when flies are least numerous and active.

Discussion.—Screwworm appears mostly in the South and Southwest where it may cause 50 percent of the normal annual livestock losses. The screwworm has been eradicated from the Southern United States east of the Mississippi River.

(10) **Ticks.**—Several kinds may be found on horses. The most common ones are the winter tick, *Dermacentor albipictus;* the lone star tick, *Amblyomma americanum;* and the spinose ear tick, *Otobius megnini.*

Symptoms.—The symptoms are lowered vitality and itching; animals rub and scratch infested parts.

Treatment.—To control winter and lone star ticks, use the same treatments that are used for lice. For the control of spinose ear ticks, apply a 5 percent coumaphos dust inside the ears, or spray inside the ears with an aerosol bomb containing 2.5 percent ronnel. Repeat treatments as necessary.

Prevention and control.—Treatment with insecticides will control ticks on horses and protect them against reinfestation for several weeks.

Discussion.—Ticks appear mostly in the South and West. They reduce vitality of horses and may spread piroplasmosis and African horsesickness.

HORSEMANSHIP

For greatest enjoyment, a horseman should have the proper tack and clothing and learn to ride correctly. Some of the riding equipment that horsemen need and some of the principles of good horsemanship are discussed in this section.

Tack

Tack includes all articles of gear, or equipment, that are used on or attached to riding and driving horses. Each horse should have his own saddle, bridle, halter, and lead shank so they can be adjusted to fit.

Superior quality tack usually is cheaper in the long run. With proper care, it will last for many years. Some common items of tack are discussed in the following sections.

Bridles and hackamores

Lightweight bridles and bits usually indicate competent horsemen and well-mannered horses. Bridles may be either single or double. A single bridle is equipped with one bit, whereas a double bridle is ordinarily equipped with both a snaffle bit and a curb bit, two headstalls, and two pairs of reins. Only one rein is used with western bridles.

All bridles should be properly fitted, and the headstall should be located so that it neither slides back on the horse's neck nor pulls up against his ears. The cheek straps should be adjusted in length so the bit rests easily in the mouth without drawing up the corners. And the throatlatch should be buckled loosely enough to permit the hand, when held edgeways, to pass between it and the horse's throat.

The bosal hackamore and the hackamore bit-bridle are used on horses with tender mouths and as training devices for western horses.

The bosal hackamore has a pair of reins and an ordinary headstall that holds in place a braided rawhide or rope noseband knotted under the horse's jaw. It is an excellent device for controlling a young horse without injuring his mouth and is used extensively in training polo and cow ponies.

62

When properly adjusted, the hackamore should rest on the horse's nose about 4 inches from the top of the nostrils, or at the base of the cheek bones. It should also permit the passage of two fingers held edgeways between it and the jaw.

The hackamore bit-bridle is a "fake" bridle; it has the shanks on each side but no mouthpiece.

The kind of bridle or hackamore used will depend on the horse's training and intended use. Figures 58 and 59 show the most common types of bridles and hackamores.

Bits

The bit is **the most important** part of the bridle. In fact, **the chief use of the** other parts of the bridle is **to hold the bit in place in the** horse's mouth. **The bit provides communication** between the rider **or driver and the** horse.

Figures 60, **61, and 62** show the most common types of **bits. There are many variations** on each of **these types.**

The proper **fit and adjustment of** the bit is very important. **It should rest** easily in the mouth and be **wide enough** so it will not pinch the cheeks or **cause wrinkles** in the corners of

BRIDLES

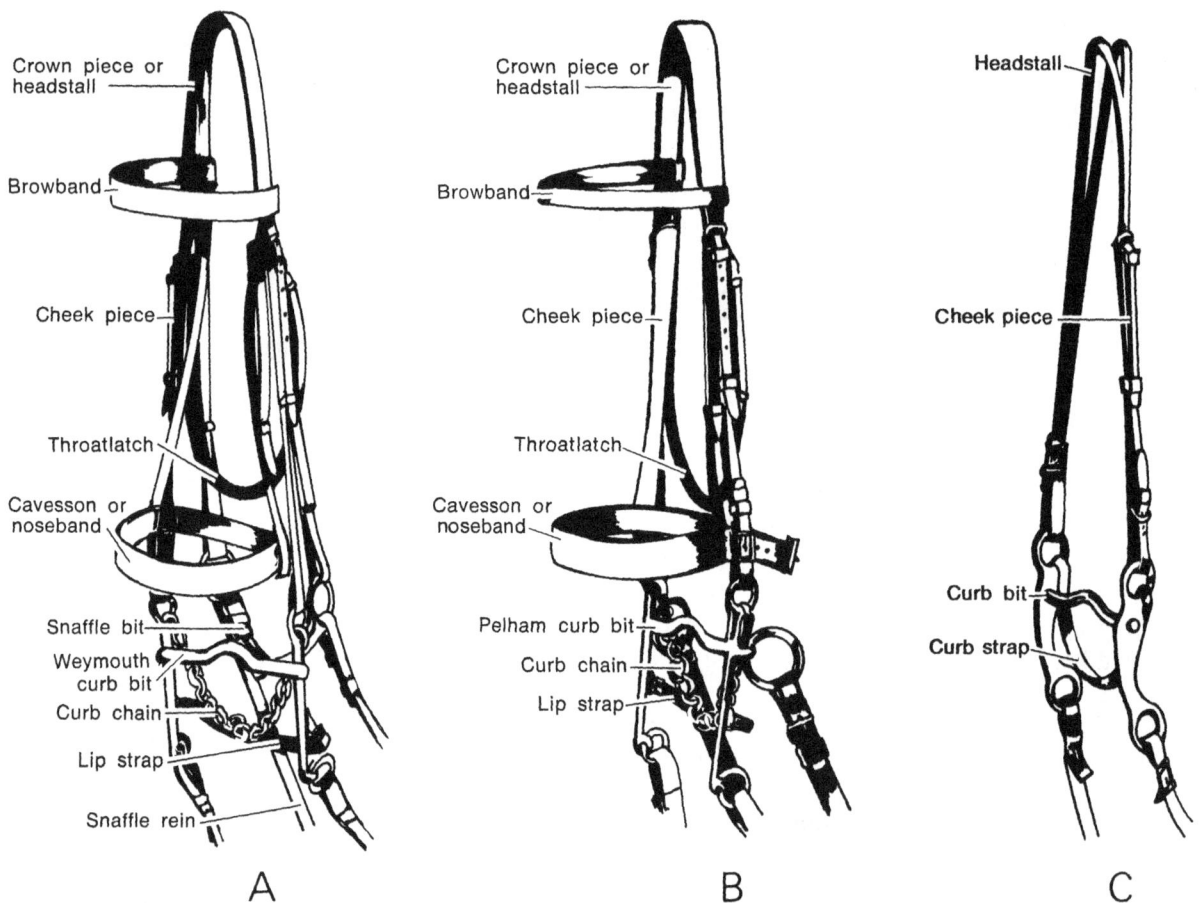

BN-37791

FIGURE 58.—Three types of bridles. (A) Weymouth bridle—a double-bitted, **double-reined bridle** used in showing three- and five-gaited horses; (B) Pelham bridle—a single bitted, double-**reined bridle used** on hunters, polo ponies, and pleasure horses; (C) One ear, or split ear, bridle—a bridle often used **on working stock horses.**

HACKAMORES

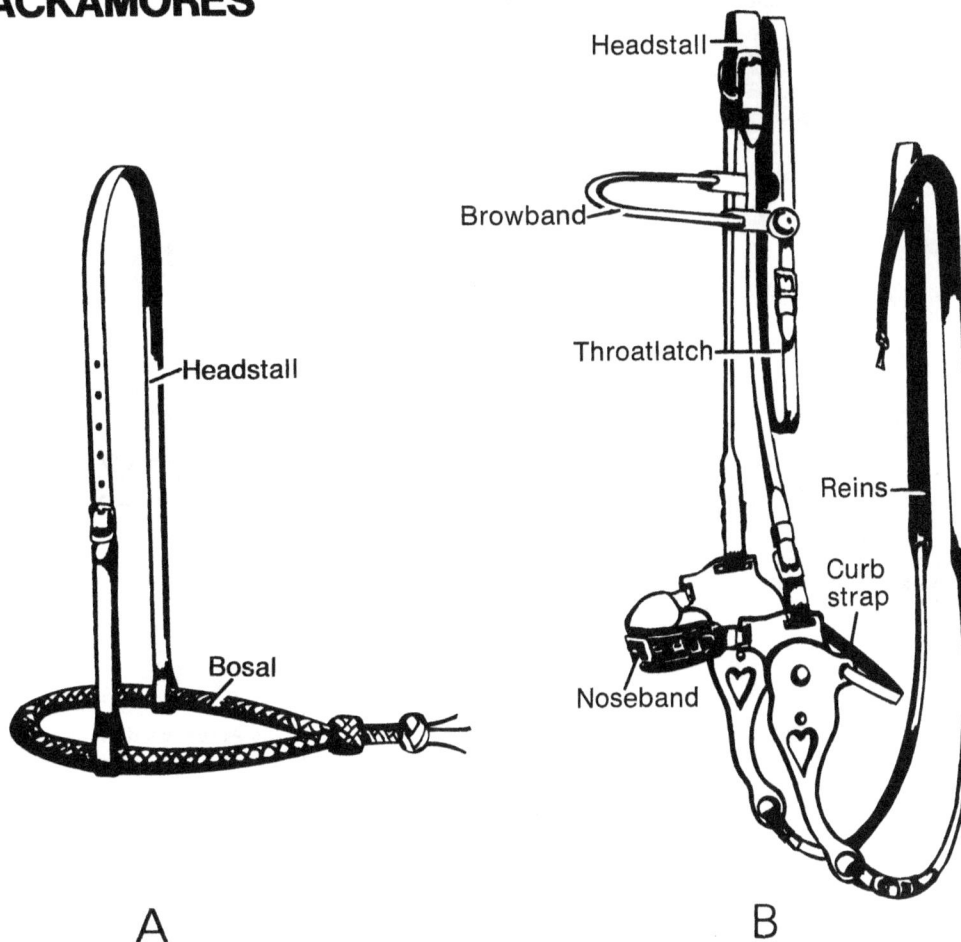

FIGURE 59.—**Two types of hackamores.** (A) Bosal hackamore—a popular hackamore for breaking horses; (B) Hackamore bit-bridle—**a hackamore with** a removable mouthpiece that is used on western cow ponies and on young horses when they **are being broken, because it** eliminates the possibility of injuring the mouth.

the mouth. As a rule, a curb-type bit rests lower in the mouth than a snaffle. All bits should have large rings or other devices to prevent them from passing through the mouth when either rein is drawn in turning the horse.

The following points about bits should be remembered:

• Usually, the snaffle bit is used when a horse is started in training.

• The hunting, or egg butt, snaffle is used on hunters and jumpers.

• The curb bit is a more severe bit than the snaffle and it may be used either alone or with the snaffle.

• The Pelham bit is one bit that is used with two reins and a curb chain. It is a combination of a snaffle and a curb bit and is used in park or pleasure riding and hunting.

• The Weymouth bit combined with a snaffle bit is known as a bit and bradoon.

• Western bits are similar to the curb bit but they have longer shanks and are larger. Usually, they are used with a solid leather curb strap but sometimes they have a small amount of chain in the middle of the leather curb strap.

Saddles

The English and western saddles are the two

ENGLISH RIDING BITS

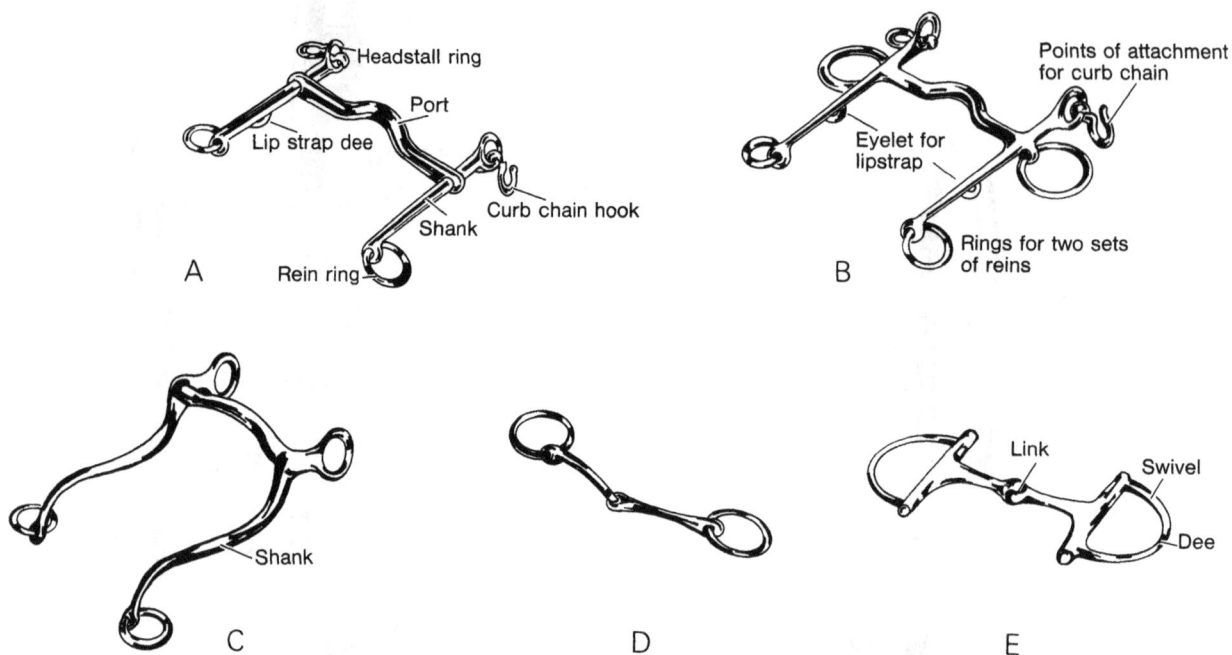

FIGURE 60.—Five common types of English riding bits. (A) Weymouth curb bit—a bit used along with a snaffle bit in a Weymouth bridle for three- and five-gaited horses; (B) Pelham curb bit—a bit used in a Pelham bridle for hunters, polo ponies, and pleasure horses; (C) Walking horse bit—a bit often used on Walking Horses; (D) Snaffle bit—the most widely used of all bits; (E) Dee race bit—a bit often used on Thoroughbred racehorses.

WESTERN RIDING BITS

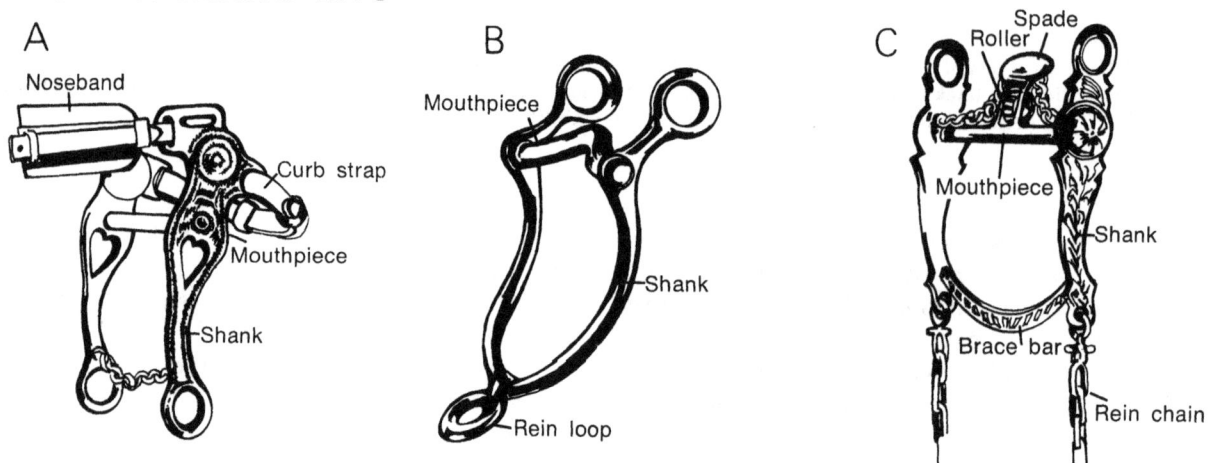

FIGURE 61.—Three common types of western riding bits. (A) Hackamore bit—a bit used on most cow ponies; (B) Roper curved cheek bit—a bit used on many roping horses; (C) Spade mouth bit—a bit used on many stock horses.

DRIVING BITS

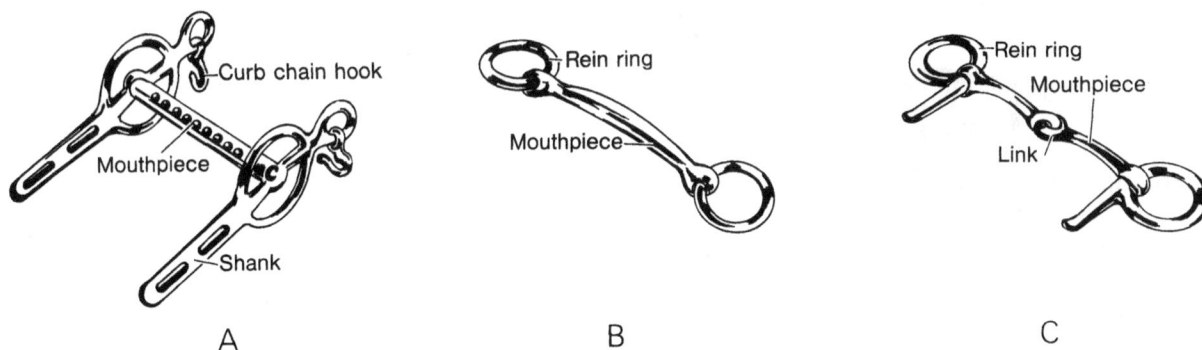

FIGURE 62.—Three common types of driving bits. (A) Liverpool bit—a curb bit used on heavy harness horses; (B) Bar bit—a bit used on trotting harness horses that carry checkreins and are driven with a strong hand; (C) Half-cheek snaffle bit—a bit used on harness racehorses, roadsters, and fine harness horses.

most common types, but individual styling within the types may vary considerably.

English saddle.—English saddles include the flat types that are modified specifically for pleasure riding, training, racing, jumping, or polo. The English saddle (fig. 63) is characterized by its relatively flat seat and its generally light weight.

The following points should be remembered about English saddles:

• When an English saddle is used on a show horse, use a white web or linen girth.

• A saddle blanket usually is not necessary with an English saddle.

• For English pleasure riding or showing, use an English saddle and a double bit or Pelham bridle.

• For hunting and jumping, use a forward seat English saddle and a hunting snaffle or Pelham bit.

Western saddle.—A western saddle (fig. 64) is the common saddle used by cowboys and western stockmen. The essential features are a steel, light metal, or wooden tree; a pommel, topped by a horn for roping, and a cantle (the height of the pommel and cantle vary according to the uses to which the saddle is to be put and the personal preference of the rider); a comparatively deep seat; heavy square or round skirts; a double cinch, usually, but a single cinch may be used; and heavy stirrups that may be hooded or open. A western saddle is designed to give comfort for all-day riding and provide enough strength to stand up under the strain of calf roping. The average western saddle weighs 35 to 40 pounds.

Clothes for Riders

In general, riding clothes seldom change in style. Moreover, they are utilitarian. Peg-top breeches, for example, provide plenty of seat room. Close fitting legs eliminate wrinkles that might cause chafing. Chamois leather linings inside the knees and calves keep the muscles of the legs from pinching under the stirrup leathers and increase the firmness of the leg grip. Boots or jodhpurs protect the ankles from the stirrup irons. And high boots also keep the breeches from snaring on objects along the trail, shield the trouser legs from the saddle straps and the horse's sides, and protect the legs from rain and cold. For the most comfortable ride, wear either regulation or jodhpur type breeches made to order.

The time of day, the kind of riding horse, and the class in which shown at horseshows

Pommel
Cantle
Seat
Skirt
Panel
Stirrup bar
Stirrup iron
Tread of stirrup iron
Flap
Stirrup leather

Panel
Flap
Sweat flap
Billets

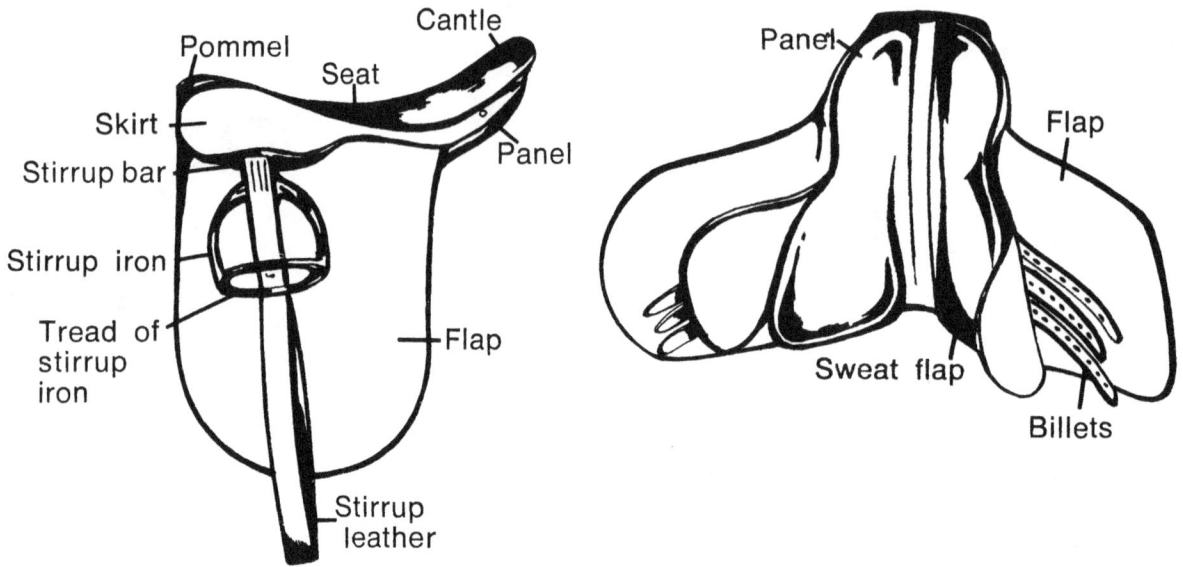

FIGURE 63.—An English saddle: Left, upright position; right, the underside.

BN–37801

Horn
Fork
Cantle
Skirt
Pommel
Seat
Wool lining
Skirt
Back housing or back jockey
Rope strap
Lace string
Lace strings
Front jockey and seat jockey, one piece
Dee ring
Dee ring
Fender or sudadero
Leather flank girth billet
Front tie strap or cinch strap
Stirrup leather keeper
Stirrup leather
Stirrup

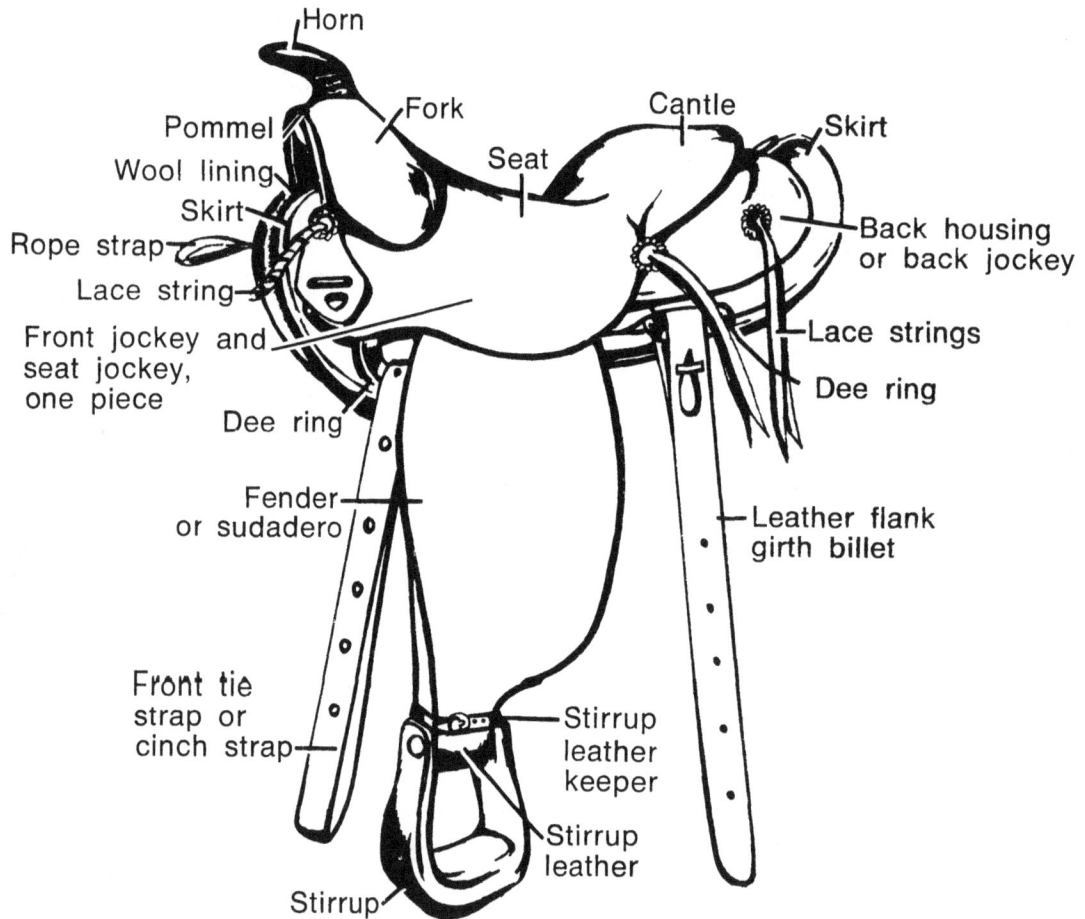

FIGURE 64.—A western saddle.

BN–37802

determine the riding attire. In addition to selecting proper clothes, well-groomed and experienced riders place emphasis on fine tailoring, good materials, and proper fit. Also, when riding a saddle horse, do not wear gaudy colors, excess jewelry, or sequins except in parade classes.

For information on clothes for riders for specific show classes see the official rule book of the American Horse Shows Association.

Appropriate riding clothes for the most common occasions are as follows:

English riding

(1) **Informal park or school riding, morning or afternoon classes.**

Coat.—Any conservative color, tweeds or checks.

Jodhpurs or breeches.—Jodhpurs of gabardine, whipcord, or cavalry twill in colors to match or to contrast with the coat; Kentucky style breeches with bell bottoms and no flare at the hips.

Vest.—Optional; light, solid color or tattersall check.

Shirt.—Man's shirt, white or colored, broadcloth or oxford cloth.

Neckwear.—Four-in-hand tie or bow tie.

Hat.—Saddle derby to match jodhpurs or coat.

Boots.—Black or brown strap or elastic jodhpur boots.

Gloves.—Optional; leather gloves to blend with habit.

Jewelry and other accessories.—Cuff links, tie pin, belt; spurs of unrowelled type and whip or crop optional.

(2) **Semiformal, afternoon or evening classes.**

Coat.—Gabardine, wool gabardine, dress worsted, or other men's-wear materials; inverted pleats in back; dark colors preferred; in summer, linen or tropical worsted.

Jodhpurs or breeches.—Jodhpurs of same material as coat to make a matching riding habit; Kentucky style breeches with bell bottoms, no flare at the hips, and no cuff.

Vest.—Solid color or tattersall check.

Shirt.—Man's shirt in white or light color to match suit.

Neckwear.—Man's four-in-hand tie to match or contrast with the coat.

Hat.—Saddle derby to match suit.

Boots.—Black or brown jodhpur boots.

Gloves.—Optional; leather in a natural shade or to match suit.

Jewelry and other accessories.—Tie clasp, cuff links, belt; spurs and riding whip optional.

(3) **Formal evening riding.**

(a) **Five-gaited horse.**

Coat.—Black or midnight blue tuxedo style riding coat with one button in front and inverted pleats; men usually wear a dark suit instead of a tuxedo.

Jodhpurs or breeches.—Material and color to match coat.

Vest.—Any solid color to match habit.

Shirt.—Man's shirt.

Neckwear.—Four-in-hand or bow tie.

Hat.—Saddle derby.

Boots.—Black jodhpur boots with tuxedo; brown or black with a suit.

Gloves.—Leather gloves to match habit.

Jewelry and other accessories.—Cuff links and tie pin; gaited riding whip, crop, and spurs optional.

(b) **Three-gaited horse.**

Coat.—Tuxedo model in black or midnight blue; shawl collar with satin lapels; soft pastel colored coats also can be worn; white coat in summer. Equitation classes must wear a dark tuxedo style coat with a silk top hat in the evening and a matched suit with a derby in the daytime.

Jodhpurs or breeches.—Material and color to match coat; satin stripe down outside of jodhpurs.

Vest.—Optional; white pique vest or cummerbund.

Shirt.—Formal style, white, stiff-front tuxedo; shirt with wing collar and pleated front.

Neckwear.—Black, white, or midnight blue bow tie.

Hat.—Silk top hat.

Boots.—Black leather or patent leather jodhpur boots.

Gloves.—Leather gloves to match habit.

Jewelry and other accessories.—Formal shirt studs; walk-trot stick optional.

Western riding

Coat.—Coats and jackets usually not worn except in bad weather; tailored equitation suits may be worn (matching shirt and pants).

Pants.—Western cut pants of gabardine, cotton twill, cavalry twill, or wool worn with chaps, shotgun chaps, or chinks; conservative color and well tailored.

Vest.—Optional; leather or cloth.

Shirt.—Western type; color to match or contrast with western pants; solid or patterned fabric acceptable; long sleeved.

Neckwear.—Knotted kerchief, dogger type tie, choker, or silk scarf tied ascot style and tucked into open neck of shirt.

Hat.—Western hat, felt or straw.

Boots.—Western boots.

Gloves.—Optional; leather.

Jewelry and other accessories.—Hand carved belt and western belt buckle; carry a rope or riata; if closed reins are used in trail and pleasure horse classes, carry hobbles; spurs optional.

Hunting and jumping

(1) Hunting (informal).

Coat.—Black oxford or tweed.

Jodhpurs or breeches.—Jodhpurs with peg and cuff or breeches; colors of brick, tan, buff, or canary.

Vest.—Optional; hunting yellow or tattersall.

Shirt.—Stock shirt or ratcatcher.

Neckwear.—Choker, stock, or ratcatcher tie.

Hat.— Brown or black hunting derby; hunting cap if 18 years old or less.

Boots.—Black or brown boots; high or jodhpur.

Gloves.—Brown leather gloves or rain gloves of string.

Jewelry and other accessories.—Stock or choker pin, hunting crop, and spurs with straps that match boots.

(2) Hunt seat equitation.

Coat.—Oxford or tweed hunt coat; black or other conservative color.

Jodhpurs or breeches.—Buff, brick, or canary breeches.

Vest.—Optional; canary with black coat.

Shirt.—Stock shirt.

Neckwear.—White stock or choker.

Hat.—Hunting derby; hunting cap if 18 years old or less.

Boots.—Black or brown hunt boots.

Gloves.—Optional.

Jewelry and other accessories.—Stock pin worn straight across on a stock tie or choker; spurs of unrowelled type and crop or bat optional.

(3) Member of a hunt (formal).

Coat.—Black hunt coat of melton or heavy twill; may wear a black coat of shadbelly or other cutaway-type scarlet hunt livery; collar should be same material and color as the coat unless the rider has been invited to wear hunt-club colors, in which case the collar should conform to hunt livery.

Jodhpurs or breeches.—Buff, brick, or canary with black coat; men wear white breeches if they wear a scarlet coat.

Vest.—Buff or yellow; hunt colors if hunt-club member.

Shirt.—White stock shirt.

Neckwear.—White stock fastened with a plain gold safety pin worn straight across stock.

Hat.—Silk hunting hat; hat guard required with scarlet coat or black shadbelly; staff members and juniors wear hunt caps; adults wear a derby with a hat guard when a black coat is worn.

Boots.—Regular hunting boots of black calf with tabs; black patent leather tops permissible for women; brown tops for men on the staff.

Gloves.—White or yellow string rain gloves or brown leather gloves.

Jewelry and other accessories.—Sandwich case, flask, and regulation hunting whip; spurs of heavy pattern with a moderately short neck, preferably without rowels and worn high on the heels.

Boot garters.—Plain black or black patent leather with patent leather boot tops; brown with brown boot tops; white with white breeches.

(4) Jumping.

Coat.—Any color of hunt coat in solid or check; jumping coat may be of any informal forward seat type.

Jodhpurs or breeches.—Breeches of a color contrasting to coat.

Vest.—Checkered or solid color.

Shirt.—Man's shirt; ratcatcher shirt when stock is worn.

Neckwear.—Stock or four-in-hand tie.

Hat.—Hunting derby or hunt cap.

Boots.—Black or brown hunting boots.

Gloves.—Optional.

Jewelry and other accessories.—Stock pin and belt; jumping bat and spurs optional.

Other riding occasions

(1) **Side saddle forward seat for hunting.**—Silk hunting hat; hat guard required; dark melton habit with matching skirt; black boots without tops; spurs are optional; white or colored rain gloves, neckwear, coat collar, vest, sandwich case, and flask are the same as for a member of a formal hunt.

(2) **Side saddle show seat.**—Habit of dark blue, black, or oxford gray with matching or contrasting skirt; black jodhpur boots; four-in-hand or bow tie; white shirt; hard derby; white or pigskin gloves.

(3) **Plantation walking horse** (Tennessee Walking Horse).—Clothes should be the same as those worn for riding three- or five-gaited horses; men can wear a soft felt hat; women seldom wear a hat.

Riding a Horse

Mounting

Before mounting always check the cinch, or saddle girth, for tightness and the stirrup straps, or leathers, for length. Mount from the left, or "near," side. Figures 65, 66, and 67 show the correct way to mount, and the correct holding of the reins, in Western and English riding.

Seat

Figures 68 and 69 show the correct riding seat for a three-gaited horse, a five-gaited horse, a plantation walking horse, a western horse, and a hunter and jumper.

Rules of good horsemanship

Horsemen should always practice safety and show consideration for other riders. The following are some of the rules of good horsemanship:

• Approach a horse on his left. Never walk or stand behind a horse unannounced; let him know you are there by speaking to him and placing your hand on him. Otherwise, you may get kicked.

• Pet a horse by first placing your hand on his shoulder or neck. Do not dab at the end of his nose.

• When leading a horse, grasp the reins close to the bit on his left side.

• Walk a horse to and from the stable; this prevents him from running to the stable and from refusing to leave the stable.

• Make sure the saddle blanket or pad is clean and free of any rough places to prevent a sore back.

• Check the saddle and bridle, or hackamore, before mounting. The saddle should fit just back of the withers; it should not bear down on or rub the withers, but also it should not be placed too far back. The girth should be fastened snugly and should not be too close to the forelegs. Be sure that the bridle, or hackamore, fits comfortably and that the curb chain, or strap, is flat in the chin groove and fastened correctly.

• Mount and dismount from the left side. The horse must be made to stand still until the rider is properly seated in the saddle or has dismounted.

• Sit in the correct position for the style of riding.

• Keep the proper tension on the reins; avoid either tight or dangling reins.

• Keep the hands and voice quiet when handling a horse. Never scream, laugh loudly, or make other noises that will upset the horse. Do not slap a horse with the ends of the reins when he is excited.

FIGURE 65.—(A) In English riding, take the reins in the left hand and place the left hand on the withers. Grasp the stirrup leather with the right hand and insert the left foot in the stirrup. Swing around to face the horse, hop off the right foot, grasp the cantle with the right hand, and spring upward and over. Settle into the saddle and slip the right foot into the off stirrup without looking down. (B) In western riding, take the reins in the left hand and place the left hand on the horse's neck in front of the withers. Keep the romal or the end of the reins on the near side. Grasp the stirrup with the right hand, place the left foot in the stirrup with the ball of the foot resting securely on the tread. Brace the left knee against the horse, grasp the saddle horn with the right hand, and spring upward and over. Settle into the saddle and slip the right foot into the off stirrup.

HOLDING THE REINS WESTERN STYLE

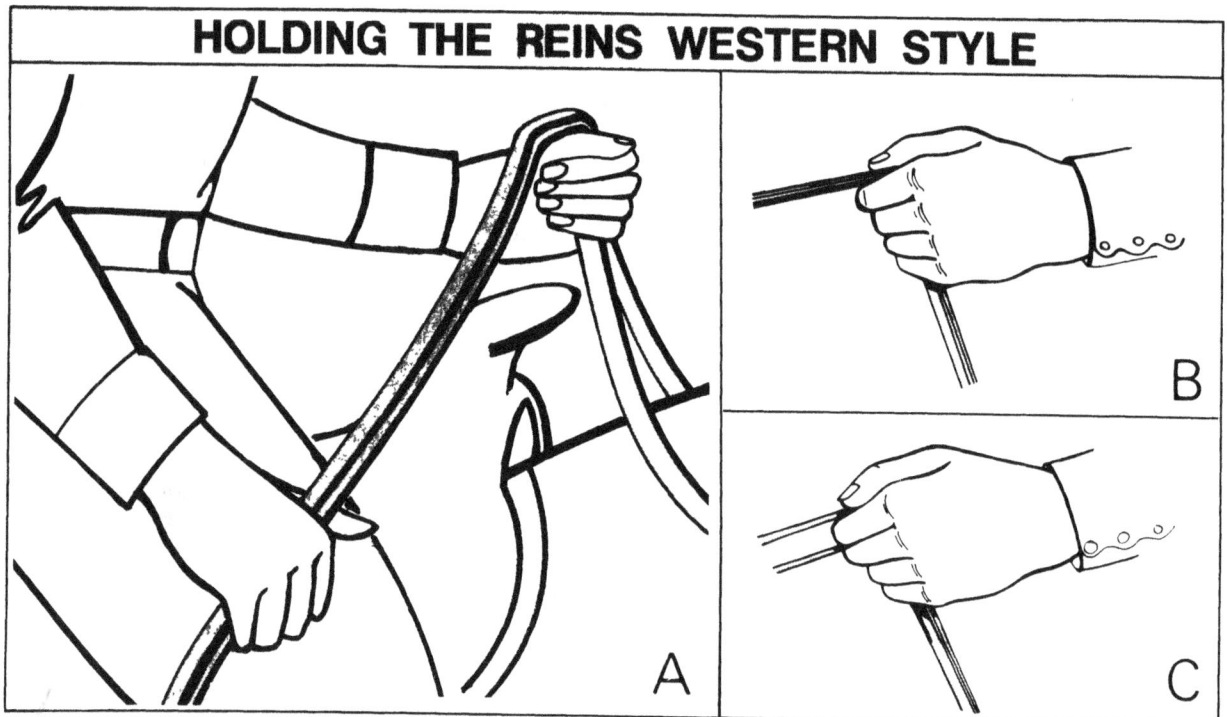

FIGURE 66.—Holding the reins western style: (A) Only one hand can be used and hands cannot be changed; (B) The hand must be around the reins with no fingers between reins unless split reins are used; (C) When using split reins, one finger between reins is permitted.

HOLDING THE REINS ENGLISH STYLE

DOUBLE-REIN BRIDLE

Right Hand

R. Snaffle

R. Curb

Bight

Left Hand

Arms held horizontal to elbow

L. Curb

L. Snaffle

REINS IN TWO HANDS

Left Hand

R. Snaffle
R. Curb
L. Curb
L. Snaffle

Arm held horizontal to elbow

REINS IN ONE HAND

SINGLE-REIN BRIDLE

Left Hand

Right Hand

REINS IN TWO HANDS

Left Hand

REINS IN ONE HAND

BN–37796

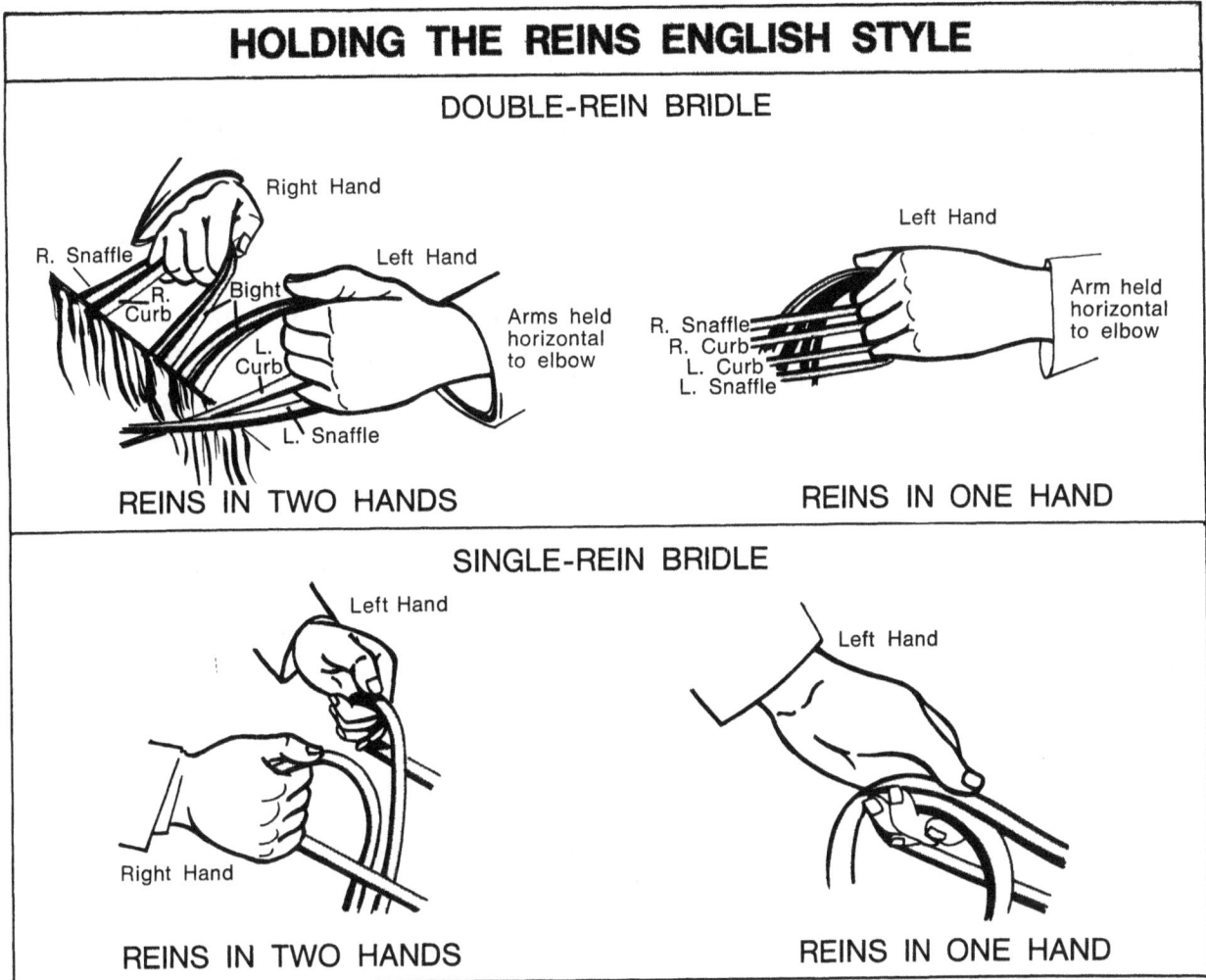

FIGURE 67.—Holding the reins English style: Top, double-rein bridle; bottom, single-rein bridle.

• Warm up a horse gradually; walk him first and then jog him slowly.

• Keep to the right side of the road except when passing. Yield the right-of-way courteously.

• Walk a horse across bridges, through underpasses, on pavements and slippery roads, and when going up or down hill. Do not race a horse; he will form bad habits and may get out of control.

• Slow down when making a sharp turn.

• Keep a horse moving when a car passes. If he stops, he may back into the passing vehicle.

• Anticipate such distractions as cars, stones, paper, trees, bridges, noises, dogs, and children.

• Vary the gaits; do not force a horse to take a rapid gait such as a canter, rack, or trot for more than a half mile without allowing a breathing spell.

• Keep a horse under control at all times if possible. Try to stop a runaway horse by sawing the bit back and forth to break his stride and his hold on the bit; in an open space, pull one rein hard enough to force the horse to circle.

• Be firm with a horse and make him obey. At the same time, love and understand him and he will be a good friend.

• Never become angry and jerk a horse; a bad-tempered person can make a bad-tempered horse.

• Lean forward and loosen the reins if a horse rears. Do not lean back and pull because the horse might fall over backward.

• Pull up the reins of a bucking horse and keep his head up.

• Loosen the reins and urge a horse forward with your legs if he starts backing. Do not hold the reins too tightly when a horse is standing still.

• Walk a horse at the end of a ride to let him get cool.

• Do not allow a horse to gorge on water when he is hot; allow a warm horse to drink only a few swallows at a time.

• Do not turn a horse loose at the stall entrance. Walk into the stall with him and turn him around so that he is facing the door. In a tie stall, make certain that the horse is tied securely with a proper length rope.

• Groom a horse thoroughly after each ride.

• Wash the bit thoroughly before it is hung in the tack room. Remove hair and sweat from the saddle and girth before putting them on the rack.

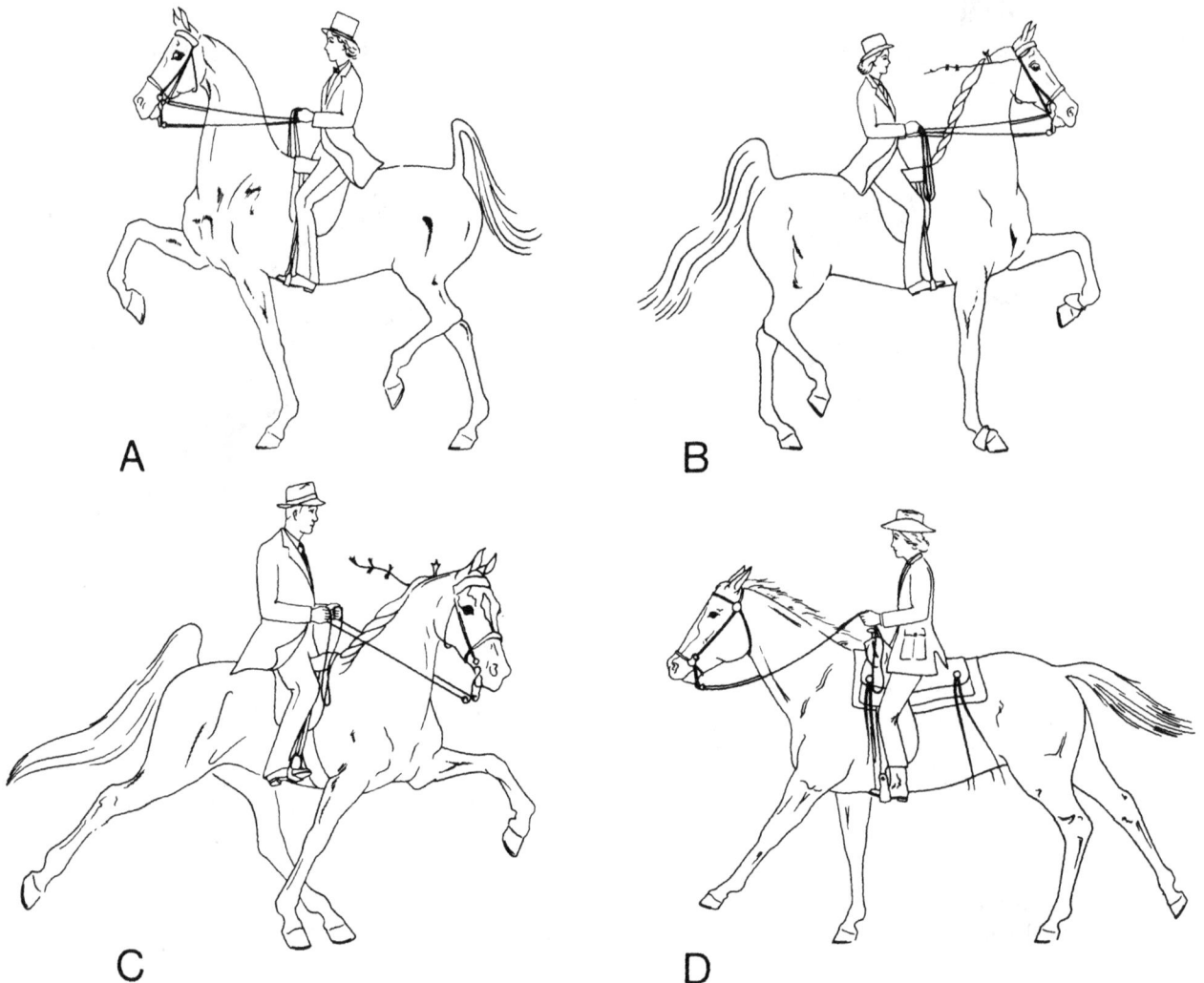

FIGURE 68.—(A) Correct show seat and riding attire for a three-gaited horse; (B) Correct show seat and riding attire for a five-gaited horse; (C) Correct show seat and riding attire for the running walk; (D) Correct seat and riding attire for western riding.

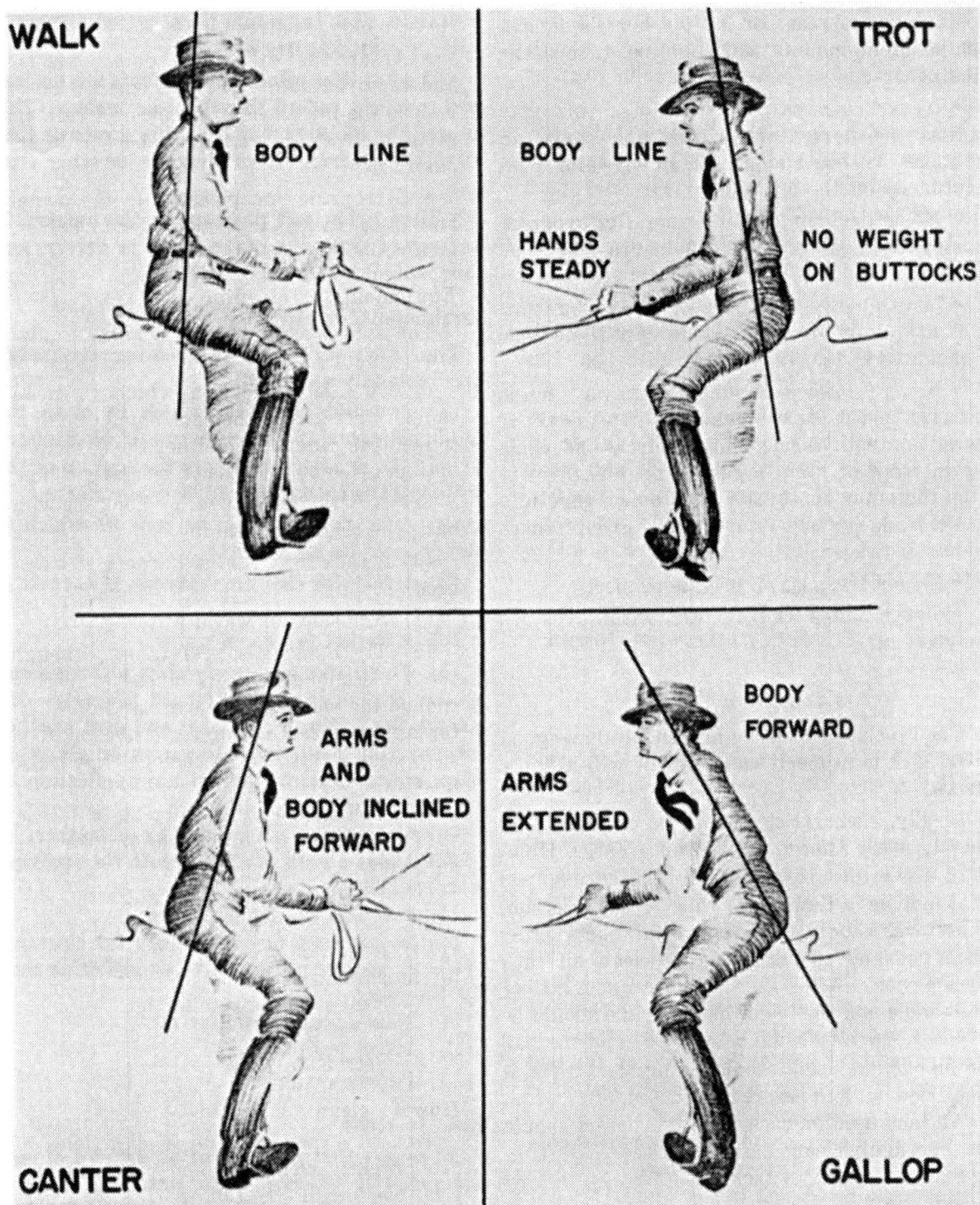

WALK

BODY LINE

TROT

BODY LINE

HANDS
STEADY

NO WEIGHT
ON BUTTOCKS

ARMS
AND
BODY INCLINED
FORWARD

BODY
FORWARD

ARMS
EXTENDED

CANTER

GALLOP

BN–37809

FIGURE 69.—The correct saddle position for hunting and jumping: Note the position for the walk, the trot, the canter, and the gallop; the proper seat for all gaits requires the head to be erect, the heels down, the weight uniformly balanced, the back concave, and the knees and thighs gripping the saddle.

• When riding in a group, keep about 5 feet apart when abreast or a full horse's length behind other mounts when in line, to prevent kicking.

• Never rush past other riders; this may startle the horses and riders and cause an accident. Instead, approach slowly and pass cautiously on the left side.

• Never dash up to another horse or group of horses at a gallop; this can injure riders or horses.

• Wait quietly when a rider must dismount. Do not start moving again until he has remounted and is ready to go.

• Never chase a mounted runaway horse because this will only make him run faster; if possible, another rider should circle and come up in front of him. In case a rider is thrown, stop the other horses and keep quiet; generally the loose horse will return to the group where he can be caught.

• Do not trespass on private property.

• Leave gates closed; otherwise, livestock may get out.

Caring for Tack

Good tack is expensive and should have good care. If it is properly cared for, it will last for years.

Ideally, each article should be cleaned thoroughly every time it is used on a horse. However, the owner or caretaker of pleasure horses may not have time to do this. A busy person, therefore, should clean the vital parts after each use and then thoroughly clean all tack once a week. After each use, the underside of the saddle and the inside of the bridle should be cleaned; the bit should be washed; and the pad or blanket, if used, should be brushed after it has dried out and before it is reused.

All tack used on race and show horses should be thoroughly cleaned after each use.

Proper cleaning of tack will—

• Extend the life of leather and metal.

• Make leather soft and pliable.

• Help keep the horse comfortable. He will get fewer saddle and harness sores than he will from dirty, crusted, or stiff leather and less

irritation and infection than he will from a rusty, moldy, or dirty bit.

• Assure that minor tack defects are noticed and repaired before they become serious. This lessens the likelihood of breaking a rein or line, girth, girth strap, stirrup leather, or other vital part.

• Give pride and pleasure in the ownership and use of tack; the horse, rider or driver, and tack will all look good.

Equipment for cleaning

The following items of cleaning equipment are commonly used:

(1) A saddle rack on which to clean the saddle. Preferably, the rack should be designed to hold the saddle with either the seat up or the bottom up so both sides can be easily cleaned.

(2) A bridle rack, peg, or hook on which to hang the bridle for cleaning.

(3) A rack for cleaning harness, if harness is used.

(4) A bucket for warm water.

(5) Three sponges, preferably, although one sponge is enough if it is rinsed properly—one sponge for washing off sweat and dirt, another for applying leather preservative or glycerine soap, and a third for occasional application of neat's-foot or similar oil.

(6) A chamois cloth for drying off leather.

(7) About a yard of cheese cloth for applying metal polish.

(8) A flannel rag for polishing.

(9) Saddle soap or castile soap for cleaning.

(10) A leather preservative or glycerine soap for finishing.

(11) Neat's-foot or similar oil.

(12) Metal polish.

(13) Petroleum jelly.

How to clean

To assure that all parts of all articles of tack are properly cleaned, some practical order of cleaning should be followed. Any order that works is satisfactory.

Once a week all leather should be washed with saddle soap or castile soap as described in the section on washing the saddle and then neat's-foot oil or other leather dressing should be lightly applied. Do not use too much oil; it will darken new leather and soil clothing.

Wooden parts of equipment may be sanded, varnished, and waxed whenever necessary.

The following order of cleaning is suggested for the saddle, bridle, and saddle pad or blanket:

The saddle.—Clean the saddle as follows:

(1) Remove the girth and clean it first, the same way the rest of the saddle is cleaned.

(2) Turn the saddle upside down and wash the panel (the part of the saddle that touches the horse's back) and the gullet (the underside center of the saddle). Use a sponge that has been wetted in warm water and wrung out to apply saddle soap to the leather. Rub the leather well to work up a stiff lather that will remove sweat and dirt before it hardens. Wash until clean.

(3) Turn the saddle over and wash the rest of it the same way.

(4) Dry the saddle with a chamois.

(5) Dampen a clean sponge slightly and apply leather preservative or glycerine soap without suds to all parts of the saddle.

The bridle.—Clean the bridle as follows:

(1) Wash the bit in warm water.

(2) Clean the leather parts the same way the saddle was cleaned.

(3) Use a cheesecloth to apply metal polish to all metal parts of the bridle and then use a flannel cloth to polish them. If the bridle is not to be used for several days, clean and dry the bit and then apply a light coat of petroleum jelly to keep it from pitting or rusting.

The blanket or pad.—Clean blankets and pads as follows:

(1) Hang up or spread out blankets and pads to dry.

(2) When dry, brush off hair and dried sweat.

After cleaning.—Handle tack as follows after cleaning:

(1) Store all tack in a cool, dry place.

(2) Hang the bridle on its rack so all parts drape naturally without bending.

(3) Put the saddle on its rack.

(4) Cover the saddle, bridle, and harness (if harness is used).

Grooming a Horse

Proper grooming is necessary to keep a horse attractive and help maintain his good health and condition. Grooming cleans the hair, helps keep the skin functioning naturally, lessens skin diseases and parasites, and improves the condition and fitness of the muscles.

Grooming should be rapid and thorough but not so severe it makes the horse nervous or irritates his skin. Horses that are kept in stables or small corrals should be groomed thoroughly at least once a day. When horses are worked or exercised, they should be groomed both before and after the work or exercise.

Wet or sweating animals should be handled as follows:

(1) Remove the tack as fast as possible, wipe it off, and put it away.

(2) Remove excess water from the horse with a sweat scraper and then rub him briskly with a grooming or drying cloth to dry his coat partially.

(3) Cover the horse with a blanket and walk him until he is cool.

(4) Allow the horse to drink two or three swallows of water every few minutes while he is cooling and drying.

Equipment for grooming

The following articles of grooming equipment are commonly used:

(1) A hoof pick to clean the feet.

(2) A rubber or metal curry comb to groom horses that have long thick coats and to loosen scurf and dirt in the hair.

(3) A body brush to brush the body. This is the principal tool used in grooming.

(4) A dandy brush to remove light dirt from the skin and to brush the mane and tail. The dandy brush is made of stiff fiber, usually about 2 inches long.

(5) A mane and tail comb to comb out a matted mane and tail.

(6) A sweat scraper to remove excess water from wet or sweating animals.

(7) A grooming cloth to wipe and polish the coat and for other miscellaneous cleaning. The grooming cloth can be made from old towels or blankets. It should be about 18 to 24 inches square.

How to groom

To assure that the horse is groomed thoroughly and that no body parts are missed, follow a definite order of grooming. This may vary according to individual preference, but the following order is most common:

The feet.—Use a hoof pick to clean the feet. Work from the heel toward the toe. Thoroughly clean the depressions between the frog and the bars. Inspect the feet for thrush and loose shoes.

The body.—To groom the body, hold the curry comb in the right hand and the brush in the left hand. Start on the left side of the horse and follow this order: neck, breast, withers, shoulders, foreleg down to the knee, back, side, belly, croup, and hindleg down to the hock.

At frequent intervals, clean the dust and hair from the brush with the curry comb. Knock the curry comb against some solid object to free it of dirt.

Curry gently and in small circular strokes, but brush vigorously. Do not use the metal curry comb below the knees or hocks, about the head, or over body prominences. Also, the metal curry comb should not be used on horses that have been clipped recently or that have a thin coat of hair.

Brush the hair in the direction it grows. Brush with care in the regions of the flanks, between the fore and hindlegs, at the point of elbows, and in the fetlocks.

After grooming the left side of the horse, transfer the brush to the right hand and the curry comb to the left hand and groom the right side.

The head, mane, and tail.—Brush the head and comb and brush the mane and tail. Use the body brush on the head. Brush the mane and tail downward, using either the body brush or the dandy brush.

Clean the tail by combing upward with a mane and tail comb, cleaning a few strands of hair at a time, or by picking and separating a few hairs at a time by hand. Wash the mane and tail occasionally with warm water and soap.

Miscellaneous cleaning.—Use the grooming cloth to wipe about the ears, face, eyes, nostrils, lips, sheath, and dock; to give a final polish to the coat; and to dry or ruffle the coat before it is brushed.

Checking the grooming.—Rub the fingertips against the natural lay of the hair. If the coat and skin are not clean, the fingers will get dirty and gray lines will show on the coat where the fingers passed. Inspect the cleanliness of the ears, face, eyes, nostrils, lips, sheath, and dock.

Cleaning the grooming equipment.—Wash the grooming equipment with warm water and soap often enough to keep it clean. Disinfect it as a precaution against the spread of disease.

Clipping and shearing.—Besides routine grooming, horses should be clipped as often as needed. Clip the long hairs from the head, the inside of the ears, on the jaw, and around the fetlocks. A wad of cotton may be put in the horse's ears to cut down on noise from the clippers and to prevent hair from falling in his ears.

According to custom, certain breeds are clipped and sheared in different hair cuts and hair styles. These are illustrated in figure 70.

Showing a Horse

To have success in showing horses, an exhibitor must know the rules of the class and the correct showing techniques.

Performance classes for horses are so numerous and varied that it is not practical to describe them here. Instead, the showman should refer to the official rule book of the American Horse Shows Association and to the rules printed in the programs of local horse shows.

Breeding classes are discussed here. They are shown "in hand," which means the horses are exhibited wearing a halter, preferably, or a bridle. The halter should be clean, properly adjusted, and fitted with a fresh looking leather or rope lead. If the horse is shown wearing a bridle, the exhibitor should not jerk on the reins hard enough to injure the mouth.

The following practices are recommended for showing in hand, or at halter.

(1) Train the horse early.
(2) Groom the horse thoroughly.
(3) Dress neatly for the show.
(4) Enter the ring promptly and in tandem

The natural appearing mane and tail of the Arabian.

The tightly braided mane and the docked and set tail of the Hackney.

Typical mane and tail treatment of the Tennessee Walking Horse.

The clipped or roached mane and the cut, set and shaved tail of the 3-gaited American Saddle Horse.

The shortened, pulled mane and the tightly braided tail of the polo pony. This type of mane treatment is also often seen on Quarter Horses.

The full mane with braided foretop and first lock and the full water spout tail of the 5-gaited American Saddle Horse.

The usual mane and tail treatment of the Quarter Horse. The mane is clipped with the foretop and a tuft of hair at the withers left. The tail is shortened and shaped by pulling.

The braided mane and the thinned tail and braided dock of the hunter.

BN-37803

FIGURE 70.—Common haircuts and hairstyles for different breeds and uses of horses.

78

when the class is called. Line up at the location indicated by the ringmaster or judge unless directed to continue around the ring in tandem.

(5) Stand the horse squarely on all four feet with the forefeet on higher ground than the hindfeet if possible. The standing position of the horse should vary according to the breed. For example, Arabians are not stretched, but American Saddlers are trained to stand with their front legs straight under them and their hindlegs stretched behind them. Other breeds generally stand in a slightly stretched position, somewhat intermediate between these two examples. When standing and facing the horse, hold the lead strap or rope in the left hand 10 to 12 inches from the halter ring. Try to make the horse keep his head up.

(6) Unless the judge directs otherwise, the horse should first be shown at the walk and then at the trot. Move the horse as follows:

(a) Reduce the length of the lead strap or rope by a series of "figure 8" folds or by coils held in the left hand. Hold the upper part of the lead strap or rope in the right hand and lead from the left side of the horse. If the horse is well-mannered, give him 2 to 3 feet of lead so he can keep his head, neck, and body in a straight line as he moves forward. But keep the lead taut so the horse is always under control. Do not look back.

(b) The exhibitor should keep the horse's head up and briskly move him forward in a straight line for 50 to 100 feet as directed.

(c) At the end of the walk, turn to the right. That is, the exhibitor should turn the horse away from himself and walk around the horse. If the horse is turned toward the exhibitor, the horse is more likely to step on the exhibitor. Make the turn in as small a space as practical, and as effortless as possible. When showing at the trot, bring the horse to a

walk and move him slightly in the direction of the exhibitor before turning.

(d) The exhibitor should lift his knees a little higher than usual when he is showing in the ring.

(e) Trail the horse with a whip if it is permitted and desired. Most light horses are given early training by trailing with the whip but usually they are shown without this aid. If a "trailer" is used, he should follow at a proper distance. The distance should not be so near he might get kicked but not so far he would be ineffective. The trailer should keep the animal moving in a straight line, avoid getting between the judge and the horse, and always cross in front of the horse at the turn.

(7) Walk the horse down about 50 feet and walk back; then trot down about 100 feet and trot back. To save time, the judge may direct that horses be walked down and trotted back, which is a proper procedure. After the horse has been walked and trotted, stand him promptly in front of the judge. After the judge has made a quick inspection, move to the location in the line indicated by the ringmaster or judge.

(8) Keep the horse posed at all times; keep one eye on the judge and the other on the horse.

(9) When the judge signals to change positions, the exhibitor should back the horse out of line, or if there is room, turn him to the rear of the line and approach the new position from behind.

(10) Try to keep the horse from kicking when he is close to other horses.

(11) Keep calm; a nervous showman creates an unfavorable impression.

(12) Work in close partnership with the horse.

(13) Be courteous and respect the rights of other exhibitors.

(14) Do not stand between the judge and the horse.

(15) Be a good sport; win without bragging and lose without complaining.

BREED REGISTRY ASSOCIATIONS

The names and addresses of some of the breed registry associations for some of the breeds of horses are as follows—

American Albino Association, Inc., Box 79, Crabtree, Oregon 97335
American Association of Owners and Breeders of Peruvian Paso Horses, P.O. Box 371, Calabasas, California 91302
American Buckskin Registry Association, P.O. Box 1125, Anderson, California 96007
American Connemara Pony Society, Route 2, Featherbed Lane, Ballston Spa, New York 12020
American Gotland Horse Association, R.R. #2, Box 181, Elkland, Missouri 65644
American Hackney Horse Society, 527 Madison Avenue, Room 725, New York, N.Y. 10022
American Morgan Horse Association, Inc., Box 265, Hamilton, New York. 13346
American Mustang Association, Inc., 997 South Douglas Street, Calimesa, California 92320
American Paint Horse Association, P.O. Box 12487, Fort Worth, Texas 76116
American Paso Fino Pleasure Horse Association, Inc., Arrott Building, 401 Wood Street, Pittsburgh, Pennsylvania 15222
American Quarter Horse Association, P.O. Box 200, Amarillo, Texas 79105
American Remount Association, 20560 Perris Boulevard, Perris, California 92370
    (Half-Thoroughbred Registry)
American Saddle Horse Breeders Association, 929 South Fourth Street, Louisville, Kentucky 40203
American Shetland Pony Club, P.O. Box 2339, West Lafayette, Indiana 47902
Appaloosa Horse Club, Inc., Box 403, Moscow, Idaho 83843
Arabian Horse Club Registry of America, One Executive Park, 7801 Belleview Avenue, Englewood, Colorado 80110
Cleveland Bay Society of America, White Post, Virginia 22663
Galiceno Horse Breeders Association, Inc., 708 Peoples Bank Building, Tyler, Texas 75701
Hungarian Horse Association, Bitterroot Stock Farm, Hamilton, Montana 59840
International Arabian Horse Association, 224 East Olive Avenue, Burbank, California 91503
Jockey Club, The, 300 Park Avenue, New York, N.Y. 10022
    (Thoroughbred horses)
Missouri Fox Trotting Horse Breed Association, Inc., P.O. Box 637, Ava, Missouri 65608
Morocco Spotted Horse Cooperative Association of America, Route 1, Ridott, Illinois 61067
Palomino Horse Association, Box 128, Chatsworth, California 91311
Palomino Horse Breeders of America, P.O. Box 249, Mineral Wells, Texas 76067
Pinto Horse Association of America, Inc., Box 3984, San Diego, California 92103
Pony of the Americas Club, Inc., P.O. Box 1447, Mason City, Iowa 50401
Spanish Mustang Registry, Inc., Cayuse Ranch, Oshoto, Wyoming 82724
Tennessee Walking Horse Breeders' Association of America, P.O. Box 286, Lewisburg, Tennessee 37091
United States Trotting Association, The, 750 Michigan Avenue, Columbus, Ohio 43215
    (Standardbred horses)
Welsh Pony Society of America, Inc., 202 North Chester Street, West Chester, Pennsylvania 19308

HORSE MAGAZINES

The horse magazines publish news and other information of special interest to horsemen. The names and addresses of some of these magazines are listed as follows—

American Shetland Pony Journal, Box 2339, West Lafayette, Indiana   47906

Appaloosa News, Box 403, Moscow, Idaho   83843

Arabian Horse News, Box 1009, Boulder, Colorado   80302

Arabian Horse World, 2650 East Bayshore, Palo Alto, California   94303

Arizona Horseman, The, 2517 North Central Avenue, Phoenix, Arizona   85004

Arizona Thoroughbred, 3723 Pueblo Way, Scottsdale, Arizona   85251

Backstretch, The, 19363 James Couzens Highway, Detroit, Michigan   48235

Blood Horse, The, P.O. Box 4038, Lexington, Kentucky   40504

British Columbia Thoroughbred, The, 4023 East Hastings Street, North Burnaby, British Columbia, Canada

Chronicle of the Horse, Middleburg, Virginia   22117

Equestrian Trails, 10723 Riverside Drive, North Hollywood, California   91602

Florida Horse, Box 699, Ocala, Florida   32670

Harness Horse, Telegraph Press Building, Harrisburg, Pennsylvania   17101

Hoof Beats, 750 Michigan Avenue, Columbus, Ohio   43215

Hoofs and Horns, 1750 Humboldt Street, Suite 21, Denver, Colorado   80218

Horse and Rider, Gallant Publishing Co., 116 East Badillo, Covina, California   91722

Horse and Show, Box 386, Northfield, Ohio   44067

Horse Lover Magazine, The, Box 914, El Cerrito, California   94530

Horse Show, 527 Madison Avenue, New York, N.Y.   10022

Horse Show World, P.O. Box 39848, Los Angeles, California   90039

Horse World, P.O. Box 588, Lexington, Kentucky   40501

Horseman, 5314 Bingle Road, Houston, Texas   77018

Horsemen's Journal, 425 13th Street, N.W., Washington, D.C.   20004

Horsemen's Review, P.O. Box 116, Roscoe, Illinois   61073

Horsemen's Yankee Pedlar, Box 297, North Wilbraham, Ludlow, Massachusetts   01067

Lariat, The, Route 6, 14239 N.E. Salmon Creek Avenue, Vancouver, Washington   98665

Maryland Horse, The, P.O. Box 4, Timonium, Maryland   21093

Morgan Horse, The, Box 265, West Lake Moraine Road, Hamilton, New York   13346

National Horseman, The, 933 Baxter Avenue, Louisville, Kentucky   40204

Northeast Horseman, Box 47, Summer Street, Hampden Highlands, Maine   04445

Oregon Thoroughbred Review, 1001 North Schmeer Road, Portland, Oregon   97217

Owners and Breeders Registry, The, Drawer XX, Livingston, Alabama   35470

Paint Horse Journal, The, P.O. Box 12487, Fort Worth, Texas   76116

Palomino Horses, Box 249, Mineral Wells, Texas   76067

Pinto Horse, P.O. Box 3984, San Diego, California   92103

Pony of Americas Club Official Magazine, P.O. Box 1447, Mason City, Iowa   50401

Quarter Horse Digest, Gann Valley, South Dakota   57341

Quarter Horse Journal, Box 9105, Amarillo, Texas   79105

Rider and Driver, Box 254, Iola, Wisconsin   54945

Saddle and Bridle, 2333 Brentwood Boulevard, St. Louis, Missouri   63144

Southern Horseman, The, P.O. Box 5735, Meridian, Mississippi   39301

Spanish Mustang News, The, 2005 Ridgeway, Colorado Springs, Colorado   80906

Tack 'N Togs, The Miller Publishing Co., P.O. Box 67, Minneapolis, Minnesota   55440

Thoroughbred of California, Box 750, 201 Colorado Place, Arcadia, California 91006
Thoroughbred Record, P.O. Box 580, Lexington, Kentucky 40501
Trail Rider, The, Trail Rider Publications, Chatsworth, Georgia 30705
Turf and Sport Digest, 511–513 Oakland Avenue, Baltimore, Maryland 21212
Voice of the Tennessee Walking Horse, Voice Publishing Co., P.O. Box 6009, Chattanooga,
    Tennessee 37401
Washington Horse, The, 13470 Empire Way, South, Seattle, Washington 98178
Welsh News, 1770 Lancaster Avenue, Paoli, Pennsylvania 19301
Western Horseman, The, 3580 North Nevada Avenue, Colorado Springs, Colorado 80907

PRECAUTIONS

Pesticides used improperly can be injurious to man, animals, and plants. Follow the directions and heed all precautions on the labels.

Store pesticides in original containers under lock and key—out of the reach of children and animals—and away from food and feed.

Apply pesticides so that they do not endanger humans, livestock, crops, beneficial insects, fish, and wildlife. Do not apply pesticides when there is danger of drift, when honey bees or other pollinating insects are visiting plants, or in ways that may contaminate water or leave illegal residues.

Avoid prolonged . inhalation of pesticide sprays or dusts; wear protective clothing and equipment if specified on the container.

If your hands become contaminated with a pesticide, do not eat or drink until you have washed. In case a pesticide is swallowed or gets in the eyes, follow the first aid treatment given on the label, and get prompt medical attention. If a pesticide is spilled on your skin or clothing, remove clothing immediately and wash skin thoroughly.

Do not clean spray equipment or dump excess spray material near ponds, streams, or wells. Because it is difficult to remove all traces of herbicides from equipment, do not use the same equipment for insecticides or fungicides that you use for herbicides.

Dispose of empty pesticide containers promptly. Have them buried at a sanitary land-fill dump, or crush and bury them in a level, isolated place.

NOTE: Some States have restrictions on the use of certain pesticides. Check your State and local regulations.

www.ingramcontent.com/pod-product-compliance
Lightning Source LLC
Chambersburg PA
CBHW080338270326
41927CB00014B/3281